90 MEDITATIONS FOR YOUTH

Alfred P. Klausler

Let the words of my mouth and the meditation of my heart be acceptable in Thy sight, O Lord, my Rock and my Redeemer.

Psalm 19:14

Concordia Publishing House
St. Louis, Missouri

FOREWORD

Editor Alfred P. Klausler knows that deep in the hearts of today's teen-agers there is a sincere desire for moments of quiet, reflection, and meditation.

As author of 90 MEDITATIONS FOR YOUTH Pastor Klausler has given to inquiring youth a book that will be treasured and often used by modern teens. Those young people who through God's grace are members of our Christian church will find this book of meditations especially meaningful. Between its covers are interesting, educational, and relevant helps to devotion and contemplation on the Church Year, the Disciples, numerous characters of the Scriptures, of friends and relations, and of things and possessions.

I have known Alfred P. Klausler for more than a dozen years as a youth worker. God has given this author a deep and significant understanding of young people. His ability to communicate ably with youth through the printed word becomes immediately discernible through the 90 brief meditations presented.

Every subject is apt and appropriate. Each one has in it enough appeal and enough genuine interest to open wide the wonder gate of youth and to stimulate them to good meditation. Some of the subjects treated are unusually excellent; for example: to think of Martha not for her being busy in the kitchen, but rather for the truly great confession of faith in Jesus she made at the tomb of her brother Lazarus.

The author, even though an editor and correspondent for many important publications, has written 90 MEDITATIONS FOR YOUTH in simple, plain, easy-to-read, yet dignified language. Young people will not be satisfied with reading only one or two chapters, but will want to read more, and some repeatedly. This rising generation must think carefully, meditate often, and draw heavily upon the resources of the Word. Klausler's book will be helpful.

Because young people love variety, the author has skillfully woven into many of the chapters new ways to practice the art and discipline of Christian meditation. At times he suggests in a key sentence what to think about. Also, he suggests to write down the names of friends, and subjects or ideas that are pertinent to the meditation itself.

This book will be appreciated all the more because of the variety of meditation procedure employed.

Everyone who knows God or who wants to know Him will be enriched and strengthened through 90 MEDITATIONS FOR YOUTH. It can become for all youth a real aid in life's struggle. We are happy to see this type of literature, for we believe, with the author, that every youth wants a quiet moment in his busy life, yet not boring. Happily, Alfred P. Klausler, in 90 MEDITATIONS FOR YOUTH, helps to make this possible.

MARCUS RIEKE
Youth Director
American Lutheran Church

April 1959

CONTENTS

ON MEDITATING

In the hectic pace of modern living most of us have little or no time to sit back to meditate or think. Days in high school are crowded with dozens of activities, not to mention the class-work which must be done if good marks are to be obtained. Television, dates, church activities, and community responsibilities, as well as part-time jobs, hardly leave time for that needed eight hours of sleep.

As a result God is oftentimes crowded out of our lives. We say our prayers in a hurried way. We dash to church, and the service is half over before we have caught our breath. When there is a little time to read the Bible, we are too tired to concentrate.

Despite all this hurrying and rushing, every Christian must take the time and meditate on that most important of all relationships — the relationship with God.

To think, to ponder, to meditate on spiritual matters is highly necessary.

How does one meditate? Really, it's quite simple. At first meditating may seem difficult, even rather out of date in this age of electronics. Don't let our jet-propulsion age stop you. Set up a pattern for meditating. Begin today.

The first thing to remember is that meditation must have God and the Cross at the center. Read a portion of the Bible. After you have done that, quietly ask yourself these three questions:

What does God say?
What does God say to me?
What does God want me to do?

This is just one pattern for a meditation. Great Christian men and women of all ages have developed innumerable patterns of thinking in a systematic way about God. Once you begin the practice of meditation (start with five minutes of meditation), you will discover your spiritual life immensely enriched, and your prayers will acquire greater significance for yourself.

Naturally, your reading of Holy Scripture will also take on new meaning.

The meditations in this book deal with a variety of subjects. They are about God, about people of the Old and the New Testament, about your personal relationships, about your problems and situations which may disturb or puzzle you. They do not fall into a set pattern. As a matter of fact, many of them may violate some rules of meditation. However, the over-all object of these meditations is to start you thinking spiritually.

Some of these meditations have been adapted from meditations written by Christian youth attending youth camps, workshops, retreats, schools. Practically all of the themes of these meditations were suggested to me by young people who took time to think about God.

The meditations on "Personal Chastity" and on "My Country" were adapted from litanies first appearing in *The Student Prayer Book*.

All Bible passages appear in the Revised Standard Version unless otherwise noted.

There is an air of expectancy, an undercurrent of waiting, which makes Advent such a meaningful time of the year. There is only one page left on the calendar. Soon that page will be torn off, and a new year will have dawned once more. But in the Christian's way of measuring time a new year starts with the first Sunday in Advent. When that Sunday dawns, he knows that in less than a month all of Christendom will rejoice over the birth of the Savior.

Advent is a time of penitence. The dominant color in the church chancel is violet, a reminder that Christians must sorrow over their sins and admit their unworthiness to receive the Christ Child. In the light of the shining purity of this Child, come from heaven, man suddenly seems low and mean.

Advent is a time to think about the Day of Judgment, that time when the world will crash and disappear in a consuming heat. The time of this end is unknown. However, it certainly will come, for Christ has said that it will surely come. When the world seems safe, when all is going well, when life stretches out before everyone as a glorious road, then the Day will come as a thief in the night. Jesus Christ comes at this moment to judge the living and the dead.

Advent is a time of preparation, therefore, for the coming of the Child to Bethlehem and to our lives. Advent is a time of preparing for the last hours, when Jesus Christ appears in our midst.

Oh, come, oh, come, Emmanuel,
And ransom captive Israel
That mourns in lonely exile here
Until the Son of God appear.
Rejoice! Rejoice! Emmanuel
Shall come to thee, O Israel.

The innkeeper returned grumbling to his bed. A couple had asked for a room in his inn. Having none, he had sent them to the stables. Now there was quiet again in the little village.

Just outside the village limits a group of shepherds had a startling experience. The heavens above them exploded with light. A heavenly messenger told them to hurry into Bethlehem because there they would find that Person for whom the world had been waiting long weary centuries.

And it was all true, the shepherds discovered. Here was the Child. Here was the mother. Here truly was the Savior of the world.

This is Christmas as it was then and as it is today.

We still journey the weary miles to Bethlehem with Mary and Joseph. We still hear the curt reply of the innkeeper, "There is no room." We still huddle out in the fields and are frightened by the heavenly burst of light. We still listen with wonder at the heavenly choir singing praise and glory to God for this amazing deed: the birth of His Son. We still hurry to the manger and with the shepherds offer our humble gifts to the Child destined to be our Savior.

This is the simple meaning of Christmas which has captured the hearts of millions of believers from Korea to Kansas and from Australia to Newfoundland: Jesus Christ has come into the world to fulfill His glorious mission of saving the sinners.

On Christmas we greet our friends and neighbors with joy. We give gifts to those who are near and dear to us. We join in the moving anthems which sing of this birth. We crowd into our churches, there to worship at the manger.

Joy to the world, the Lord is come!
Let earth receive her King;
Let every heart prepare Him room
And heaven and nature sing.

The journey had no doubt been long and arduous. For days they had pressed forward, searching for the end of their quest. They wanted to see the Being to whom that mysterious star had pointed. Many years had been spent in studying the Sacred Scriptures. Within these scrolls they had read that some day a Messiah, a Savior, would come for the redemption of all mankind.

These Wise Men, also called the Magi, finally arrived at journey's end. First they presented their problem to Herod, a wicked king who wanted no rivals. Warned by God in a dream to avoid Herod, they finally found the Christ Child. There, before the wondering eyes of His mother, they knelt and reverently presented precious gifts: gold, frankincense, myrrh. They had found the Savior, the first Gentiles to come to faith in the Savior. The shining light of the Redeemer brightened their lives.

Epiphany means simply the showing forth in glory of God's Son to mankind.

May His glory be present also in my life, child of God that I am.

Epiphany remains a glorious celebration in the Christian Church because it is an eternal reminder that the Gospel is intended for all men. It is a reminder to every Christian that the best is none too good for the Savior. Even as these Wise Men gave the best in their power, so the Christian happily and generously bestows his gifts upon the Christ Child, whose coming into the world brings joy to the world.

MY PRAYER

And bid Thy Word within me
Shine as the fairest star;
Keep sin and all false doctrine
Forever from me far.
Help me confess Thee truly
And with Thy Christendom
Here own Thee King and Savior
And in the world to come. Amen.

Lent can mean a variety of things to a variety of people. To some people it is that period of the year which heralds the coming of spring, for Lent does come when our Northern world is awakening from its winter sleep. To other people Lent is a time of going without something. Two high school students were talking in a corridor. "What did you give up for Lent, Jean?" "Oh, I gave up cupcakes during Lent."

To the Christian who cherishes the life of Christ, the season of Lent is a particularly precious time of the church year. During these forty days the Christian turns his thoughts and devotions to the sad events of Jesus' last days. The Christian contemplates the many aspects of Jesus' suffering at the hands of those who hated Him.

While a Christian could just as well concentrate during a one-week period as during forty days, still this lengthy period of time, symbolic of Jesus' forty days in the wilderness after His baptism, gives the Christian a far better opportunity to pay continuous attention to the meaning of the events of Holy Week.

Give up cupcakes for Lent? Stay away from movies during this time? No dates during Lent? The unthinking Christians could do all these things but miss the important aspect of Lent.

The supremely necessary fact to remember is that the entire world is involved in what happened to Jesus in His suffering and death. If there were no sinners, if sin had never happened, then there would be no Lent, no Calvary, no crucifixion.

As the Christian contemplates the history of Jesus' last days, he says, "Lord, it is my fault and my many sins which have caused Thee to suffer. Forgive me for bringing this pain and sorrow upon Thee. Yet I thank Thee for Thy love in laying down Thy life for my sins."

When I survey the wondrous cross
On which the Prince of Glory died,
My richest gain I count but loss
And pour contempt on all my pride.

(Here meditate
reverently on the meaning of the Cross in your life)

Forbid it, Lord, that I should boast
Save in the death of Christ, my God;
All the vain things that charm me most,
I sacrifice them to His blood.

(Here meditate
solemnly on your personal sins for which Christ died)

See, from His head, His hands, His feet,
Sorrow and love flow mingled down.
Did e'er such love and sorrow meet
Or thorns compose so rich a crown?

(Here meditate
on the sufferings of the crucified Christ on Calvary)

Were the whole realm of nature mine,
That were a tribute far too small;
Love so amazing, so divine,
Demands my soul, my life, my all. — *Isaac Watts*

(Here meditate
joyfully on the life you can give to your Savior)

Lord, have mercy upon me.
Christ, have mercy upon me.
Lord, have mercy upon me.

The glorious fact is that Christ did rise from the dead.
1 Corinthians 15:20 (Phillips)

In the cool dawn of a Palestinian morning several figures can be seen scurrying through a parklike garden. They are on their way to the tomb where has been laid the body of One they loved and believed in. The tragic events of the past days are still a harrowing memory. But as they come to the tomb, they are shocked to discover that the heavy stone placed at the entrance to the tomb has been moved away. With timid and frightened steps they enter. And there, where they expected to find the body of their Lord, they see instead an angel. Shocked and frightened, they draw back. Then they hear the divine messenger speak. "He is risen," are the amazing words. "He is not here. Do not look for His body among those who are dead. He lives. Tell others about this."

This is Easter, simply related in the Gospel story, yet the great fact which makes the Christian faith the eternal hope of those who look for certainty in this life and in the life to come.

Easter did not happen in the inflamed mind of Luke or John or Mark or Matthew. These four evangelists did not sit down together to concoct a story about a man rising from the dead. Years later St. Paul reminds his friends in Corinth that *after* His resurrection Jesus was seen by the Twelve, by James, by Cephas, and by over five hundred Christians at one time. Thus Jesus Christ did truly rise from the dead, and even as He is risen from the dead, all those who believe in Him will also rise from the dead.

MY EASTER PRAYER

Almighty God, give me always a strong faith in my risen Savior so that I may at the end of my days on this earth come to Him in the perfect peace of heaven. Amen.

The time has passed all too rapidly. It is now forty days since their Lord returned from the dead. During this time He associated with them on various occasions. He walked with two disciples on the road to Emmaus and explained to them the meaning of His life, death, and resurrection. He shamed doubting Thomas. He spoke words of comfort to all the disciples.

Now the small group accompanies Jesus to a hill outside Jerusalem. Perhaps they realize that He cannot stay with them much longer. Secretly perhaps they hope that He will change His mind and remain in their midst.

Of course, He did not do so. Their Lord reminds them once more that He must return to His heavenly Father. At the same time He reassures them that they will not be alone. They will have the divine comfort of the Holy Spirit, who will give them power to carry out the mission assigned to them by Jesus.

Then it happens so quickly that they are perhaps almost caught unawares. While Jesus is talking to them and as the last echo of His voice comes to them, they see Him lifted heavenward, and within a short space of time He is hidden from their view by a cloud.

Two men in white robes now stand before them. These are heavenly messengers with a word of comfort, a word which reassures them that Jesus will come again. The disciples return joyfully to Jerusalem and spend their time in the temple blessing God for all that had been shown to them.

The ascension of Jesus still comforts all believers because it is another proof that Jesus dwells in heaven, where every Christian will be reunited with his Lord and Savior.

MY PRAYER

O King of Glory, may I, too, dwell with Thee in heaven. Amen.

Anniversaries may be both happy and solemn occasions. The anniversary of the birthday of the Christian church is a time of happiness. Pentecost is the festival of the Christian church year when we recall the outpouring of the Holy Spirit upon the gathered disciples in Jerusalem.

Picture the scene. Perhaps the disciples wonder whether the Comforter and the Spirit of Power promised by their Savior will ever appear. Here they are alone, hated and despised by many people, ready to tell others about the Savior. Somehow they do not have the vitalizing energy so necessary to preach the Gospel. They are huddled together praying — praying that God would be with them.

Suddenly the roar and rushing sound of strong wind fills the room. Accompanying this phenomenon are the tiny tongues of flame which flicker upon the head of each person in the room.

Now they find themselves gifted with strange powers. They can speak in tongues they had never heard before. They are filled with a burning zeal to tell others about the work of Jesus Christ, who had been in their midst not so many days ago. They have courage and zeal.

The disciple who less than two months ago had cravenly denied that he was a friend of Jesus finds himself impelled to address the crowds who had gathered in the street outside the dwelling place where they were meeting. Peter preaches a tremendously moving sermon. As a result of this sermon more than three thousand people come to faith.

This is the birthday of the New Testament church, yours and mine. From that day on the march of the Christian faith has been an amazing story of the triumph of the Cross in all parts of the world.

MY MEDITATION

How can I make effective Jesus' command in Acts 1:8, "You shall be My witnesses"?

In the name of the Father and of the Son and of the Holy Ghost.

The last great festival of the Christian church year is devoted to the Triune God. For generations great theologians and philosophers have meditated on the Trinity. What sort of God do we Christians believe in? How does one explain the Triune God?

You cannot explain the Trinity. This is a divine mystery. Only in heaven will this mighty fact of our faith be made clear to all believers. There is one God, we confess with Holy Scripture. There are three Persons, we also confess with Holy Scripture. These Three are one God.

These three Persons in the Holy Trinity are distinct from one another. Each Person is equally powerful and equally eternal. Each Person receives the honor and adoration which is due the Lord of heaven and earth.

The learned Bishop Athanasius centuries ago wrote this great confession: "Of these three Persons none is the first, none the last, none the greatest, none the smallest, but all three Persons are equally eternal, equally great. . . . Yet there are not three Gods, but one God."

Even though our human minds cannot understand or fathom this mystery of the Godhead, we remain grateful to a God who is so far above us that we must bow before Him in awe and reverence. Who wants a god able to be understood by the human mind? Who desires to worship a god who is on the same level with human beings?

We glorify God for His indescribable magnificence and join with all of Christendom in singing —

Glory be to God the Father,
Glory be to God the Son,
Glory be to God the Spirit:
Great Jehovah, Three in One!
Glory, glory,
While eternal ages run! Amen.

An old guide in the Big Horn Mountains of Wyoming once said: "I like to hear people's talk around the campfire at night after a day of traveling through these mountains. Sooner or later they say they just have to believe in God." The towering splendor of the mountains and man's contrasting smallness cause people to think of God, who made all things.

Truly, God is the Creator of the mountains and the plains and the seas. All that we can see and the vast unseen world which scientists are only now beginning to explore was made by God. Before God created the heavens and the earth, there was only desolate waste. After six days of divine creative activity God had brought about a world whose wonders still captivate the imagination of mankind.

Wonderful as is the world which God created, even more wonderful is the human being, the direct handiwork of God. Who has ever successfully probed the working parts of the human brain? What scientist has ever analyzed the intricate workings of the heart? For centuries learned men have spent their entire lifetime studying the complicated process of life in the human being. It is certain this study will go on for centuries.

The more one probes the secrets of the universe the more one must sit back utterly astonished and amazed at the work of God the Father, the Creator of the world. This God is still at work. His creative activity is here and now.

MY MEDITATION

"He existed before creation began, for it was through Him that everything was made, whether spiritual or material, seen or unseen. Through Him and for Him, also, were created power and dominion, ownership and authority. In fact, every single thing was created through, and for, Him." Colossians 1:15, 16 (Phillips)

Question: How can I honor God as Creator?

For some thirty-three years a comparatively obscure man lived and walked about in the villages, cities, and countryside of a small country adjoining the shores of the Mediterranean Sea. This man spent the last three years of his life in energetic service to mankind. This man healed the sick, comforted the sorrowing, raised the dead. He talked a great deal about himself and about his purpose in life. At the end of his active years he was crucified as a common criminal.

This was Jesus Christ. He lived as a man, walked and talked as a man, experienced the emotions and problems of all men. He was still a young man at the time of His death.

He was far more than a man. In a unique way He was the Son of God. He came into this world not at the whim of God but for the supremely important task of saving mankind. He was in this world as a sinless, perfect man. He committed no sins in His thoughts, His words, His deeds. His life was spotless. When He died on the cross, He offered His life as payment for our sins. His rising from the tomb on Easter morning was final proof not only of His power over death but also that God was pleased with His Son's work of redemption.

Now everyone who believes that Jesus Christ is the Savior has the promise of heaven. Now everyone who believes that Jesus Christ is both God and man has a faith which holds him up in the most difficult times of life.

With the great Christian of the fourth century, Athanasius, we say "that we believe and confess that our Lord Jesus Christ, the Son of God, is God and Man."

MY PRAYER

My blessed Redeemer, give to me always a strong faith in Thy Person and work. Amen.

In the art of the Christian church the Holy Spirit is frequently symbolized by a dove. This picture is derived from Jesus' baptism, when the Holy Spirit descended upon Jesus in the form of a dove. The other symbol of the Holy Spirit is a shining flame or tongue of fire, which is a reminder of the amazing events of Pentecost, when the Holy Spirit entered the gathered disciples and gave them remarkable powers to be witnesses for the Lord Jesus Christ.

A dove and a flame. These two are beautiful pictures of the work of the Holy Spirit. The Spirit operates within your heart in a gentle, quiet way at times as you read God's Word or as you sit quietly in church meditating on your relationship to God. Or the Holy Spirit may enter your heart with a burning intensity so that you feel an immediate compulsion to do great things for your Savior.

The Holy Spirit brings you to faith through the precious Word and the Sacrament of Holy Baptism. As you attend the Lord's Table in fellowship with other Christians the Holy Spirit is present, gently prompting you to greater faith, filling your heart with an intense longing to be of greater service in the Kingdom.

When temptations are heavier than usual and when everything seems to be trying to turn you away from the Savior, then the Holy Spirit is present to keep you firm in the faith to which you pledged your undying loyalty at the time of confirmation. The Holy Spirit — unseen and unheard — is equally as powerful and equally as great as the Creator and the Redeemer. Never forget that His kindly presence in your life keeps you a beloved child of God.

MY PRAYER

O Holy Spirit, enter into my heart and keep me always a loyal Christian. Amen.

Peter first met Jesus through his brother Andrew. Our Lord immediately recognized the sturdy fisherman as an outstanding man. He gave him the name Peter, or "The Rock-man." Peter, one of the three favorite disciples of our Lord, was a leader among the disciples. When the disciples were confused and uncertain, Peter boldly declared, "You are the Christ." Many times Peter was the spokesman for the disciples, and quite often Jesus took him aside to give him special instructions. Peter was the first disciple to enter the open tomb on Easter morning, and he served as an important leader in the early Christian church. Peter's shining faith remains always as a glorious landmark in the New Testament.

Peter had his weaknesses. When Jesus pointed out to the disciples that the Son of God must suffer, Peter had the effrontery to criticize Jesus for saying such a terrible thing. Jesus severely rebuked him for this. His brash conduct in the Garden of Gethsemane when Jesus was arrested drew another rebuke from his Lord. Finally, of course, everyone remembers Peter's saddest hour: his denial of the Savior in the courtyard of the high priest's palace.

By the grace of God Peter remained in the fold and became a truly great apostle. How many times Peter must have echoed Paul's well-known thoughts: "My own behavior baffles me. For I find myself not doing what I really want to do but doing what I really loathe. . . . The evil I don't really want to do I find I am always doing," Romans 7:15, 19. (Phillips)

The contradictions are found in every Christian. Contradictory behavior is still an indication that Satan endeavors with all his powers to turn the Christian off the path of faith. It is also evidence that the old Adam, present in all of us, prefers evil. When this struggle becomes violent in the Christian life, then turn to —

MY PRAYER

Lord Jesus, when evil seeks to dominate me, give me strength to remain true to Thee in all my ways. Amen.

One of the gracious things which older brothers do when the younger members of the family begin to achieve prominence is to step quietly aside. They prefer to remain in the background, lending advice and encouragement, sometimes even money. They avoid the spotlight. They are known as the steady, dependable types.

James was the elder brother of the disciple John. Their father was a Galilean fisherman. Very early in Jesus' ministry the two young men left their trade to follow Jesus as His disciples.

James is always paired with John. He is also mentioned with Peter. These three were on special intimate terms with the Lord Jesus. James had the high privilege of being with Jesus on the Mount of Transfiguration, where one of the most significant events in Jesus' earthly life took place.

Through all the months and years of Jesus' ministry James was always at hand, ready to be of help wherever needed. No doubt after Jesus' ascension James went about his assigned task of preaching the Gospel with the same loyalty and devotion which had marked his years with Jesus.

The last we hear about James is from Luke: "About that time Herod the king laid violent hands upon some who belonged to the church. He killed James the brother of John with the sword," Acts 12:1, 2. This tragic and senseless murder by Herod snuffed out the life of a quiet, courageously loyal disciple who preferred to stay in the background but who was especially loved by the Savior.

Perhaps the most effective work for Jesus Christ is not done by those who are always in the public eye. The quiet, earnest Christian who remains in the background, working steadily for the Kingdom, may do an even greater service.

MY PRAYER

O God, as I work for Thee let me not seek the headlines, but let me seek Thy honor and glory first. In Jesus' name. Amen.

While John frequently refers to himself as the disciple whom Jesus loved, he also modestly refers to himself as "the other disciple." John, the brother of James, was also a fisherman on the Sea of Galilee. The son of Salome and Zebedee, devoted followers of Jesus, John compiled a long and distinguished record in the church.

John, James, and Peter were the only disciples privileged to see the raising of Jairus' daughter and the transfiguration of Jesus. They were the three present in the Garden of Gethsemane. Jesus entrusted the care of His mother to John.

John became one of the pillars of the Christian church and in his later life supervised many Christian churches in Asia Minor. Under Emperor Domitian he suffered banishment to the isle of Patmos, where he wrote that magnificent book of prophecy in the New Testament, the Revelation of St. John the Divine. After his banishment he is supposed to have returned to Ephesus. Here he lived to a great old age, loved and revered by all the Christians. He is the only disciple who did not die a violent death at the hands of the enemies of Christ.

John, who was loved by his Savior, no doubt felt a special obligation to demonstrate his love to his Lord. His Gospel is filled with many statements about the love of God in His Son. It is John who has recorded one of the greatest of all statements ever spoken by Jesus: "For God so loved the world that He gave His only Son, that whoever believes in Him should not perish but have eternal life," John 3:16.

The love which God has for us must always be reflected in our lives.

MY PRAYER

Heavenly Father, may Your love for me in Jesus always be reflected in my daily life. Amen.

His home was Bethsaida, which was also the home town of Andrew and Peter. He was an eager and searching man. He was acquainted with the Old Testament and knew what the prophets said about the coming of the Messiah. Together with many of his devout countrymen he must have looked longingly for the coming of the long-promised Savior.

This was Philip, one of the twelve disciples.

When he heard about Jesus and had heard Him talk, he was convinced that the Person of the Messiah was to be seen here and now. The moment he knew he had found the Savior he was determined to share Him with his friend Nathanael (Bartholomew). "We have found Him," Philip said. Although he was at first rebuffed, he experienced the joy of having gained a soul when Nathanael confessed his faith.

Later on Jesus tested the faith of this eager disciple. About five thousand people had followed Jesus into the hills near the sea of Galilee. The vast crowd had nothing to eat, and when Jesus asked Philip, "How are we to buy bread?" Philip replied in a worried tone, "Two hundred denarii would not buy enough bread for each of them to get a little." Philip had forgotten Jesus' ability to do the impossible. And so Philip receives the astonishing reminder that Jesus is all-powerful, when He feeds the people with five barley loaves and two fishes.

When the time came for Philip to go into the world to preach the Gospel, he went forth loyally. He had survived the early test of faith.

Each test of faith which comes to the Christian is God's way of strengthening that faith. When the storms of life become violent, that faith remains firm and strong.

MY PRAYER

Lord Jesus Christ, give me a strong and courageous faith. Amen.

Generally speaking, few people make it their ambition or dream to be a servant. In our modern society almost everyone wants to become, eventually, some kind of boss or supervisor or executive.

One of the significant facts of the New Testament is that various people who came into contact with Jesus and accepted Him as Savior were proud to be considered His servants. Paul even called himself a slave of Jesus Christ and considered this a high honor.

Biographical information about Jude is scarce indeed. He has the noble distinction of being listed as one of the twelve disciples. He may even have been a brother of Jesus. He was a devoted follower of the Savior and after the resurrection loyally traveled far and wide preaching the Gospel. Tradition has it that he did a great deal of his missionary traveling by ship. He is represented by the symbol of a ship at full sail. Jude is also thought to have been an energetic builder of churches. For this reason a second form of his symbol shows a carpenter's square and a boat hook.

Jude is the author of one of the shortest books in the Bible. Short as the letter is which he wrote to an unknown Christian church, it is a stirring call to loyalty to the Lord Jesus Christ. As a servant of the Redeemer, Jude asks all believers to remain firmly attached to the true faith.

To be loyal to a cause or to a person is a noble character trait. Sometimes such loyalty is misplaced because causes and people may prove false. Loyalty to Jesus Christ is never misplaced, for He is Truth Incarnate.

MY PRAYER

Holy Spirit, keep me always within the love of God as shown in His Son Jesus Christ. Amen.

One of the easiest ways to avoid facing facts is to doubt politely. This is a trick of the know-it-all or the one who feels he is superior to the average person. People who place all their confidence in their own brain power may look condescendingly on someone who does not have a superior intelligence. The trouble with this kind of people is that they forget there are different kinds of intelligence and that each person is a being in his own right.

Some think Nathanael was such a person who felt superior. Nathanael, whose given name was Bartholomew, made a questioning reference to Jesus when he first heard about Him. "Can anything good come out of Nazareth?" he asked when Philip told him about having found the Lord Jesus. Bartholomew quickly changed his opinion of Jesus when the Lord said to him, "Now here is a true man of Israel; there is no deceit in him!"

Overwhelmed by his meeting with Jesus, Bartholomew exclaimed, "Rabbi, You are the Son of God. You are the King of Israel."

There is no further record of Bartholomew in the New Testament except that he is listed as one of the twelve apostles. This, of course, was an exceedingly high honor. This meant that Nathanael qualified as one of the very few men who accompanied Jesus during His ministry and later saw Him after the Resurrection.

History is silent about Bartholomew. Legend states that he became a loyal and devoted missionary, finally suffering martyrdom for his Savior. His symbol is three flaying knives, for he is said to have been flayed alive and then crucified.

The power of Jesus can turn the most indifferent and the most calloused heart to Him.

FOR MEDITATION

Read John 1:43-51.

Thomas (known as the twin) then said to his fellow disciples, "Come on, then, let us all go and die with Him!" John 11:16 (Phillips)

I will never believe. John 20:25 (Phillips)

Thomas is a strange bundle of contradictions. There is so much about Thomas which resembles the confused modern person. This disciple is the type of person who believes only the evidence of his eyes. Not unless something is as clear as daylight will he accept the evidence. People like Thomas call themselves stern realists. They insist they won't be fooled by all sorts of idealistic dreaming. Very proudly they say they depend on their minds, not on their emotions.

There is another side to Thomas. When his Lord informed the disciples that He was going to Judea, where He had previously been threatened with violence, Thomas in an impulsive gesture of love said he wanted all the disciples to accompany Jesus to this death about which He had been speaking.

A strange mixture of contradictions. A doubting disciple and a loyal disciple wrapped up into one human being. Augustine, the great churchman of long ago, said of Thomas, "He doubted that we might not doubt."

After Jesus' ascension Thomas labored long and faithfully as a missionary in the lands of Parthia and Persia, possibly even reaching India, where he is supposed to have suffered martyrdom for his Lord. Thomas' doubt had been changed into glorious certainty. For this certainty he dared all for Christ.

MY PRAYER

Lord Jesus, think on me
Nor let me go astray;
Through darkness and perplexity
Point Thou the heavenly way. Amen.

Andrew, the first missionary

He brought him to Jesus. John 1:42

The first disciple to bring someone else to Jesus was Andrew. That "someone else" was his brother Simon Peter. The two brothers lived in Bethsaida, a simple village not too far from the shores of the Sea of Galilee. Andrew caught the vision of something truly glorious when he heard Jesus proclaimed as the Messiah. He spent some time with Jesus, and as soon as he had the opportunity he dashed off to find his brother. Andrew's first convert was truly a tremendous catch for the Lord.

After our Lord's resurrection Andrew continued to pursue his vigorous career as a missionary. While the historical records are indefinite, many people think that Andrew traveled to present-day Roumania and Greece. He is supposed to have been martyred on Nov. 30 in Greece. He was crucified on an X-shaped cross. To this day the Christian church observes Nov. 30 in honor of the first missionary. The church year always begins on the Sunday nearest St. Andrew's Day.

Thousands of missionaries have come and gone since the day when the first missionary brought his brother to Jesus Christ. Many of these missionaries have worked in lonely exile in distant lands. The results of their labors have frequently been insignificant from the human point of view. Other missionaries have had spectacular results from their labors. Of all the missionaries, past, present, and future, St. Andrew will always hold a special spot in the hearts of Christians everywhere. He brought his brother to Jesus.

SOMETHING TO THINK ABOUT

My life as a missionary for the Lord Jesus Christ.

He was not well liked by the community because he was a taxgatherer in the service of an unpopular government. Most of his fellow collectors had poor reputations because they were notorious as cheats or as people who tried to squeeze the last cent out of conscientious citizens. You can see him now, sitting in his tax office in Capernaum, brooding perhaps on the problems of life. He was still a young man, but apparently his future was doomed. He earned his pay in an extremely unpopular and unpatriotic job.

His name was Matthew. His name might just as well have been Outcast. Then one day Jesus of Nazareth came by his office. No doubt Matthew had already heard about Him, perhaps had met Him. Nobody and nothing could escape the attention of a tax collector. Jesus saw Matthew busy at his task. He said to him, "Follow Me." Without any hesitation "he rose and followed Him," Matthew 9:9.

Matthew became a disciple of Jesus, who scorned no man because of his job in life. When other outcasts saw Jesus' friendliness, they flocked to hear His words. This aroused the scorn and hatred of the proud and self-righteous people. Jesus became known far and wide as the Friend of sinners.

To this day Matthew is loved by Christians everywhere for at least two reasons. The first is that he followed Jesus without questioning. He heard the voice of the Savior and obeyed. The other reason for Matthew's high place among Christians is the marvelous life of the Lord Jesus which he wrote in the Gospel bearing his name.

"Follow Me" is the command which Jesus gives to this day. To those who are young in body and heart this cry comes as a special challenge. The young Christian always responds joyfully, "Lord, I shall always follow Thee!"

He is mentioned two times in the New Testament. He is listed as we would list a name today in a telephone directory or in a class roll call. There are some who would say he was the father of Judas Iscariot, the traitor. Others think he was the brother of Judas.

The name of this man is significant: James the Less. He was the son of Alphaeus. Sometimes he has been called James the Little because of his small stature. He is also referred to as James the Minor in contrast to the other James, one of the most prominent of all the disciples.

Despite this comparative anonymity one fact does stand out: James the Less was one of the Twelve. No one can take that honor from him. For two, if not three, years he was in close association with his Savior. During these years he became intimately acquainted with our Lord and learned that he had an important task assigned to him: preaching the Gospel.

Scripture tells little about this retiring disciple. The fact that he may have been either the brother or father of the betrayer is not counted against him. After all, God judges a person on the basis not of his relatives but of his relationship to God through Jesus Christ.

There is one unverified account which relates that James at the age of ninety-six was thrown from a temple pinnacle by an infuriated mob of Pharisees. He must also have been a brave man, for painters have traditionally pictured him with a club. His courage as a missionary and his love for the Lord gave him the strength to dare all for Christ. His symbol is generally three stones, typifying the manner of his death.

MY PRAYER

Dear Jesus, let me always decrease in importance because Thou must constantly increase. Amen.

The lackadaisical or halfhearted Christian sometimes does more damage to the cause of the Gospel than does the unbeliever. The non-Christian sees this unenthusiastic disciple and comes to the conclusion that there is really nothing to get excited about in the Gospel message.

In Palestine there was a party of enthusiastic Jews who hailed from Cana of Galilee. Their goal in life was to create greater patriotism among their fellow Jews. Many of these Zealots plotted to overthrow the hated oppressors, the Romans.

While the New Testament merely lists Simon as one of the Twelve, we might assume that some of this fiery patriotic feeling which was an earmark of Simon was transferred to the cause of the Gospel. No doubt when he was called by the Lord Jesus to become a disciple he became a dedicated Gospel preacher. In order to distinguish him from his fellow countryman, Simon Peter, the name Zealot was applied to Simon.

Today this Greek name for an eager, dedicated person is still used. A zealot is one who pursues a cause, advocates what he considers the most important things in the world, frequently upsets people with his earnestness. Generally speaking, people dislike being called zealots because this means they lack balance and a stable outlook. They are quite often intolerant.

However, the Lord Jesus Christ could well use disciples today like Simon the Zealot who are eager to do battle for the Kingdom. It is much better to have a dozen daringly eager disciples than an army of halfhearted followers.

Simon Zelotes' symbol is a fish on a book, a beautiful picturing of his fishing for the souls of men by means of the Gospel. He died a martyr.

MY PRAYER

My eternal Savior, may the Holy Spirit always fill me with zeal and enthusiasm for Thy Word and work. Amen.

After the tragic suicide of Judas Iscariot, the disciples called a meeting to choose his successor. Two men were nominated, Joseph Barsabas and Matthias. The lots were cast after the disciples had deliberated and prayed over the names of the men nominated. In the will of God, Matthias was elected. He became thereafter one of the Twelve.

There is no other mention of Matthias in the Bible outside the first chapter in Acts. Nothing more is heard about this disciple who became the new man in a truly closely knit group, the disciples of the Lord Jesus Christ.

Matthias means "gift of God." Certainly he was a gift from God in these trying circumstances. In later years Matthias perhaps thought many times about the strange workings of God in his life. He was taking the place of a man who had been a traitor to the Lord. Perhaps Matthias redoubled his efforts as a missionary to demonstrate that he was keenly aware of the great responsibility placed on him. He was the new man in a group which knew many more intimate details about our Lord's life. This did not upset him, for he knew Jesus as his personal Redeemer. He would live and die for Him as he journeyed to faraway countries preaching the Gospel.

Matthias, according to legend, died a martyr's death. His symbol is a double-edged axe with an open Bible, thus typifying his end.

Every Christian is a "new man" in the sense of being reborn through Holy Baptism. Every Christian learns from Matthias that it is not necessary to receive glory and praise and publicity. Every Christian knows that the main task in life is to be a good disciple of Jesus Christ.

MY PRAYER

Lord Jesus, make me a humble and unassuming disciple of Thee. Amen.

This is the scene: a road climbs tortuously through a mountain pass. The travelers stop as they reach the summit. They look longingly at the city spread out before them, its white buildings gleaming in the bright sunshine. Suddenly there is a clap of thunder. One of the men in their party, a distinguished-looking scholar, falls to the ground. They see him writhe in seeming pain. He seems to them to be listening to distant voices.

As quickly as this incident had happened it was all over. The scholar was blinded. They led him tenderly to the city, Damascus, where he had apparently been expected.

Perhaps the men in this travel party forgot the strange incident quickly. Christendom has never forgotten it; for this is the conversion of Saul.

He had left Jerusalem with the avowed purpose of getting rid of the Christians in Damascus. He hated Jesus Christ. To Saul the Redeemer was a cruel hoax foisted on the Jewish people. When Stephen spoke eloquently about the risen Christ, Saul raged and stormed. He was an important witness at the lynching of Stephen. Undoubtedly Saul felt that he was winning his battle against the great enemy of the Chosen People.

Now suddenly Saul changes. He meets Jesus Christ. He makes the shattering discovery that he has tried to make God his enemy but that God would not let him. Saul surrenders himself to the Lord Jesus Christ. He becomes Paul, a changed man, the greatest of all missionaries in the history of the church. In his surrender Paul was victorious, for he won his soul back from evil. He lived a surrendered life.

God causes amazing turnabouts in people who accept Jesus Christ as their Savior.

SURRENDERED LIVES

Jot down the name of one person you know whose life is

one of surrender to Jesus Christ. --

Write your name if you are surrendered to Christ. -----------

----

Writer of two of the most popular books of the New Testament is Luke, who wrote the gospel bearing his name and the exciting story of the beginnings of the church, the Acts of the Apostles.

The march of faith would be harder to understand if Luke had not told the world about the dramatic start of the church. The Christmas story has been doubly enriched by Luke's special touches in his gospel.

Luke was a doctor. He was also a very good reporter. By modern journalistic standards he would rate with the best. He was "inside" a dozen different happenings. He was also "inside" various countries to which he journeyed as a preacher of the Gospel and as a companion to Paul. He was a witness of the exciting experience in which the jailer at Philippi was converted. He saw his friends Paul and Silas withstand cruel treatment and then proceed to preach the Good News to their persecutors.

Luke was a friend also of Peter, for the first half of Acts is the story of Peter's adventures in preaching Christ to the world. Thus the story he tells of both Peter and Paul is, next to that of Jesus, the greatest in the history of the world. It is the story of the beginnings of the Christian church.

Luke must have been the kind of person who inspired confidence in others. His kindliness and bravery and devotion remain to this day a model for every Christian. He was the first Christian doctor, and he is honored thus by all believers.

MY PRAYER

Dear Savior, may the example of this inspired evangelist, Luke, the beloved physician, encourage me to be a good disciple throughout my life. Amen.

Take a long look at Barnabas in Acts 4. The world could use many more men like him. The Christian church certainly needs Barnabaslike Christians with increasing intensity.

Barnabas was so moved by the apostles' preaching about the resurrection that he sold a field which belonged to him and brought the money to the apostles to distribute among the needy in Jerusalem.

There's more to Barnabas. No doubt he experienced some of the bitter persecutions which were led by Paul before his conversion. Yet when Paul returned to Jerusalem after his remarkable conversion, Barnabas defended him before the fearful Christians who thought he was merely a spy trying to trap more Christians. Bravely Barnabas guaranteed the genuineness of Paul's conversion.

Thereafter Barnabas teamed up with Paul on a long evangelistic tour through Cyprus and Asia Minor. There is no doubt that Barnabas was a convincing preacher, for he had felt the power of the Gospel in his own life and had seen it at work in the life of his friend Paul.

One time Barnabas was compared with the Roman god Jupiter. Perhaps Barnabas had a magnetic, even overpowering appearance. Anyone looking at him and hearing him speak must have felt that a strange, powerful being had come to earth.

Later on Barnabas accompanied his nephew Mark in mission work. Perhaps Barnabas' strong faith encouraged Mark to write the gospel which bears his name.

As you meditate on the career of Barnabas, you almost inevitably come to the conclusion that the power of true believers is a mighty one. The Holy Spirit uses the believer to advance the Kingdom.

FOR MEDITATION

Loyalty to the Gospel is the mark of a true believer.

In the small fishing town Joppa, on the Mediterranean, Dorcas, known also as Tabitha or Gazelle, established an enviable reputation. The kind of life she lived was one which the Lord Jesus asked of His friends. Perhaps Paul had her in mind when he spoke so frequently of love and kindness. Her life was a vivid demonstration of Paul's well-known advice to the Ephesian Christians: "Be kind to one another, tenderhearted."

Dorcas no doubt had ample opportunity to demonstrate her Christian love among the womenfolk of Joppa. No doubt there were many widows in Joppa whose husbands had lost their lives in the perilous fishing trade on the Mediterranean Sea. For these poor unfortunates Dorcas sewed clothes, perhaps brought them baskets of food, and generally looked out for their welfare.

When she died, there was mourning among the faithful. The good Christians of Joppa sent a delegation to Peter, who was in a nearby town, and asked him to come immediately. Upon his arrival he quickly saw the deep affection in which Dorcas had been held. He asked to be left alone with the body of Dorcas. Then, after praying beside her, Peter issued the startling command, "Tabitha, arise." Dorcas arose and was once more among the living. This astonishing miracle was a testimony not only to the goodness of Dorcas but also to the power of God, the Lord of life and death.

To this day Dorcas is honored for the life of love she led. Many social-welfare groups in local congregations bear the name of Dorcas. Her name stands as a symbol of love which asks no reward or payment.

There are many Tabithas today. They will always be with us as long as there are Christians who sincerely believe they must "walk in love, as Christ loved us and gave Himself up for us."

MY PRAYER

Lord Jesus, help me always to live a life of love toward everyone. Amen.

About five hundred years before Christ a strange drama was enacted in a land whose ruler was harsh and tyrannical. The person who dared to face up to this king, known as Ahasuerus or Xerxes, was a lovely young girl, Esther, who became the wife of the man whose word could mean life or death to any subject.

The drama revolves around the plot of one man to get rid of the Jews who were living in captivity in Babylon. Through a clever stratagem, Haman, the plotter, persuaded the king to sign a death warrant for all the Jews.

Terror-stricken, the Jews appealed to Mordecai, Esther's guardian, for help. Mordecai appealed to Esther's pride in her Jewish ancestry, and with great trepidation Esther entered the presence of the powerful monarch who was also her husband. Within a comparatively short time Esther succeeds in persuading Xerxes to change his order and to punish Haman. Her countrymen are saved, and Esther's place in the affection of the king is truly secure. This thrilling story, as written in the book of Esther, still grips the heart.

Today such situations might strike the modern person as remote as a fairy tale. The fact is that temperamental monarchs like Xerxes did live, and the fact is that it took an immense amount of courage to face up to a man whose whims could affect the lives of hundreds of thousands. Esther had this courage because her courage came from the God she and her people worshiped faithfully through the years. This was the God of Abraham, Isaac, and Jacob. This was the God who led the Children of Israel out of Egypt. This was the God who continued to promise the coming of the Savior.

Esther's courage came from this great God, Creator of heaven and earth. With His help she was able to save a doomed nation.

MY PRAYER

O God, give me courage at all times, especially when Thy help is needed to make me brave as I face Thy enemies. In Jesus' name. Amen.

Martha has sometimes been rather unfairly accused of not caring very much about spiritual matters. Unthinking critics point out the famous incident when Martha spent the time in the kitchen preparing the meal while Mary listened to Jesus. Martha's patience was worn thin, and in a half-exasperated tone she asked Jesus to tell Mary to come and help her.

The second episode in which Martha plays an important part frequently receives the wrong emphasis. When Lazarus had died, Martha scolded Jesus for His delay in coming, "Lord, if You had been here, my brother would not have died." Forgotten is the interplay of conversation between Jesus and Martha which followed that statement. Martha said to Jesus, "I know that he will rise again in the resurrection at the Last Day." Then Jesus responds with one of the greatest New Testament statements: "I am the Resurrection and the Life; he who believes in Me, though he die, yet shall he live, and whoever lives and believes in Me shall never die." Now Jesus asks Martha the simple question, "Do you believe this?"

Martha replies with a magnificent confession of faith, a confession which has come down through the ages as a model for all Christians: "Yes, Lord; I have always believed that You are the Christ, the Son of God, the One who was to come into the world."

Instead of thinking of Martha as the woman who complained, think always of Martha as the woman who confessed her faith in a frank and forthright manner, proud of her faith in Jesus Christ, the Savior of the world.

MY PRAYER

O Lord, give me courage to confess Thee before my friends. Amen.

The Northern Kingdom of Israel was ruled by Jeroboam about 800 years before the coming of Christ.

The outward success of the kingdom fooled many people, especially those who had conveniently and comfortably shelved God in a hidden corner.

It is a time of spiritual decay. The nation's moral fiber has disintegrated. There is corruption in high places. The wealthy oppress the poor, and the cause of justice seems lost. At the same time the nation is booming with prosperity under a leader who has expanded the borders of the land and has made the nation a feared power.

One man saw through the outward prosperity. An obscure shepherd, a dresser of sycamore trees from Tekoa in the Judean desert, comes to the Northern Kingdom and speaks with the voice of God. He denounces the moral rottenness of the nation. He tells everyone within earshot of his voice that there is no justice in the land. He cries aloud that everywhere there are signs of decay. He declares in loud and ringing tones that God's people have drifted away from God. He mourns over their idolatry. He speaks with the voice of doom and tells these people they will be wiped off the face of the earth for their sins.

About twenty years after this ragged shepherd from the south had appeared in the Northern Kingdom, the nation was destroyed and its inhabitants were dragged into exile. Amos' call for repentance had drawn little response. There in lonely separation from their native soil the Israelites had time to remember Amos, the voice of God. Perhaps they recalled his words: "Seek good, and not evil, that you may live; and so the Lord, the God of hosts, will be with you," Amos 5:14.

FOR MEDITATION

How can God separate me from the worship of material prosperity.

You won't find a symbol to represent her as you do for many of the other great saints of the Christian church. But if you were to design a symbol for her, it would possibly consist of a door opening into a friendly home, with an outstretched hand of greeting.

This is Lydia, famed seller of purple in the city of Thyatira in what is now known as Anatolian Turkey. At that time Thyatira was a Roman city of the Asiatic Roman province.

When Paul came to Philippi, Lydia believed the message of the Gospel. She was baptized into the Christian faith. Her enthusiasm for the Lord Jesus Christ was so great that all the members of her household were also baptized. She became the first European convert.

Prosperous and clever as a business woman, she had no doubt a large establishment. Despite her many duties she found time to open her home to Paul and Silas. Her hospitality was warm and gracious, the kind which compelled the apostles to return again to her home when they had the opportunity. To this day Lydia's name is equated with hospitality. She is regarded everywhere as a symbol of kindliness to those who are in need of food and shelter. Her home was always a home away from home.

Christians are expected to be hospitable. "Do not neglect to show hospitality to strangers, for thereby some have entertained angels unawares," says the holy writer, Hebrews 13:2. Jesus was gracious and hospitable to the hungry multitudes. He was reluctant to send away the hungry four thousand and instead fed them. Hospitality and the love of the Savior go hand in hand. Lydia has set an immortal example for all Christians to follow.

MY PRAYER

Lord Jesus, may my hospitality always be a reflection of Thy love to me. Amen.

About sixty years before the reign of the great king David, a humble daughter of the Moabites showed love and devotion to her mother-in-law, Naomi. Tragedy had struck the family of Elimelech. He himself died, his sons died, and his wife Naomi was left both childless and lonely in the strange land of Moab.

When Naomi decided to return to her native land of Judah, Ruth, the widow of one of Elimelech's sons, accompanied her mother-in-law to the new land. Here in Judah she met and married the devout Boaz. The couple was blessed with a son, Obed, who later became the father of Jesse, David's father.

Thus this young widow, Ruth, who was not a member of the chosen race, became an ancestress of Jesus. Her name is on the great roll call of those who belonged to the ancestry of the Savior.

Ruth is gratefully remembered to this day because she was willing to leave her native land. She is remembered because of her affectionate regard for her mother-in-law. She is honored because, even though a foreigner, God placed her in the honored position of being in the noble pedigree of Jesus.

Ruth was a believer in the true God, and was willing to leave friends and native land to remain loyal to this faith. "Your people shall by my people, and your God my God; where you die I will die, and there will I be buried," Ruth 1:16, 17.

Her loyalty and love stand as a shining monument in a day when loyalty and love are all too often sneered at. Ruth's consecration is the kind every Christian must have deeply implanted in the heart and mind.

MY PRAYER

Dear Father in heaven, may my love to Thee be as dedicated and constant as was Ruth's of old. Amen.

Priscilla and Aquila were exiles from Italy because the emperor Claudius had ordered all Jews to leave Rome. Now they were living in Corinth, a city notorious for its moral corruption. None of their trials and none of the vice about them seemed to have affected them. They became acquainted with Paul, a fellow tentmaker.

What distinguished this particular tentmaker from all the others they had known in Italy and had met in their travels was his devotion to the Way. Priscilla and Aquila, fellow tentmakers with Paul, became fellow disciples with him. They opened up their home to him and spent many happy and inspiring hours listening to him expound the Word of God.

This dedicated couple made an impressive husband-and-wife Gospel team. When Paul journeyed to Syria, Priscilla and Aquila accompanied him. They did not complain about leaving behind the business they had succeeded in establishing. There is no record of either of them ever complaining about breaking up their home once more.

So thoroughly acquainted did they become with the Gospel that they were able to expound it in a remarkable manner. This was discovered by Apollos, a learned Jew, who came to Ephesus to preach the Gospel. "When Priscilla and Aquila heard him, they took him and expounded to him the way of God more accurately," Acts 18:26.

Those who complain that it takes too much effort to preach the Gospel ought to look carefully at these two tentmakers. When school life or a job seems more imporant than being a Christian, Priscilla and Aquila's devotion to the Savior will always serve as an inspiring stimulant.

MY PRAYER

Dear Lord Jesus, may I never count the cost of being Thy disciple. Amen.

There are many tragic biographies in the New Testament. Perhaps one of the saddest is that of a prominent government official who could not make up his mind about the Gospel.

Felix was the procurator of Judea. He was a trusted Roman government official. During his governorship he did many cruel deeds to the citizens of that unhappy' country of Palestine. However, he had a chance to redeem himself in the eyes of God and of the Christians in Jerusalem.

Felix was acquainted with the Way, Luke writes in Acts. Indeed he had a rather accurate knowledge of what the coming of Jesus Christ meant to sinners.

When Paul was arrested on the false charge of profaning the temple, Felix presided at the hearing. Paul spoke earnestly about sin and the Savior. His defense was so eloquent, "Felix was alarmed and said, 'Go away for the present; when I have an opportunity I will summon you,' " Acts 24:26.

Felix, so far as we know, never did come to faith. Felix never did acknowledge his sins. Felix never did accept Jesus Christ as his Savior. He could not make up his mind. He wanted to think about the Gospel a while longer, and when the right opportunity came, he would summon Paul again.

The Gospel cannot be dodged. The decision every person must make about the Redeemer cannot be postponed. When the Gospel is heard, the decision must be made immediately. Faith cannot be put off to a more convenient time. Felix stands as an everlasting symbol of a man who delayed until it was too late.

MY PRAYER

Father in heaven, send the Holy Spirit to me and to all people. Help everyone to accept the Gospel while there is still time. Amen.

Ananias, the forgotten Christian

There are no monuments or symbols honoring the man who befriended the blind and dazed Paul as he came to Damascus. Perhaps Ananias is in no need of a monument because his deed of kindness is the greatest of all monuments.

As Ananias went about his daily tasks in Damascus, he received a strange order from God, "Rise and go to the street called Straight, and inquire in the house of Judas for a man of Tarsus named Saul; for, behold, he is praying." Ananias murmured a gentle protest. After all, Saul's reputation as a murderer of Christians had penetrated the Christian colony at Damascus. Now God was asking Ananias to be kind to a man who had played an important role in the killing of Stephen.

Ananias obeyed God's command. He befriended this nationally prominent persecutor of the Christians. He called him "Brother Saul." The blinded Pharisee regained his sight and from that time on marched forward carrying the banner of the Cross to the Roman Empire.

There is no further record of Ananias in the New Testament, at least nothing of significance. He becomes the forgotten Christian. In fact, his name is frequently confused with the infamous Ananias who attempted to cheat the disciples in Jerusalem.

Most Christians may become forgotten people in the written record. They never become celebrities. They never have churches named after them. Their lives may be lived out in quiet obscurity.

The glorious fact about Ananias is his obedience to God and his kindness to a desperately lonely man. He performed this deed because he loved the Lord Jesus Christ, his Savior. So, in the final analysis, Ananias is not the forgotten Christian but the remembered child of God.

FOR MEDITATION

Read Ananias' biography in Acts 9.

No one except a Christian can appreciate the thrill and joy of reading or hearing about mission work in many lands and areas. As the stories of missionary triumphs are told in church papers, every Christian feels that the biggest joy in the world is to preach the Gospel. The missionaries in New Guinea or Taiwan or Africa are truly doing work which is of greater importance than that of diplomats or military leaders. They are, in the words of Vachel Lindsay,

"An endless line of splendor,

These troops with heaven for home." *

The joy of mission work comes not only from reading about the conquests the missionaries make for Christ. The joy of missions comes to every Christian who takes an active interest in bringing a soul to the Lord.

A prominent politician was once asked, "What is the greatest thrill you ever had?"

The newspaper correspondent expected the Congressman to say, "The excitement of winning my first election."

Instead the Congressman replied, "When I was a high school senior, my closest friend was the center on our basketball team. I admired him greatly for his sportsmanship and for his athletic ability. He was a gentleman through and through, and I was proud of his friendship. One Sunday a missionary from China spoke in our church about the joy of doing mission work. I remember the missionary telling us we could have the same joy if we would bring a soul to Christ. Well, sir, I persuaded my high school friend to hear the message of the Gospel. He became a Christian. That was my greatest thrill in life."

MY PRAYER

Dear Lord Jesus, may my joy in mission work always be strong. Amen.

* "Foreign Missions in Battle Array," by Vachel Lindsay, in *Masterpieces of Religious Verse*, edited by James Dalton Morrison. Permission granted by The Macmillan Co.

Holy God, to whose service I have dedicated my soul and life, I grieve and lament before Thee that I am so often prone to sin and so little inclined to leading a chaste and decent life in word and deed. Forgive me for being —

So attached to the pleasure of sense, so negligent of things spiritual;

So prompt to gratify my body, so slow to nourish my soul;

So greedy for present delight, so indifferent to lasting blessedness;

So fond of idleness, so indisposed for labor;

So soon to play, so late to prayer;

So brisk in the service of self, so slack in the service of others;

So lofty in my profession, so low in my practice;

So full of good intentions, so backward to fulfill them;

So delighted in impurity, so ashamed of purity;

So given to indecent thoughts and desires, so far from the clean and good;

So ready to misuse Thy great gift of sex, so reluctant to be chaste;

So eager to serve myself, so slow to be concerned about others;

So helpless apart from Thee, and yet so little willing to be bound to Thee.

O merciful God, grant me forgiveness for the sake of Thy beloved Son Jesus Christ. Amen.

MY PRAYER FOR CHASTITY

O God, keep me from degrading or belittling the personalities of others. Help me to shun dreams and thoughts and acts which will degrade me and fill my soul with all sorts of darkness and despair. May I always remember that I cannot have an unrestrained fling now and then return untouched to Thy way in later life. Lord, keep me strong. Lord, love me always. In Jesus' name. Amen.

Oh, sing to the Lord a new song; sing to the Lord, all the earth! Sing to the Lord, bless His name. Psalm 96:1, 2.

In the great cathedral there is a sudden hush as the carillon rings out the notes announcing the beginning of the worship. The vast congregation listens reverently while the organist begins a Bach prelude. Soon the mighty music of a great composition by a devout composer rolls through the cathedral, reverberates against the walls, seems to float heavenward with the prayers of the worshipers. Now the congregation joins in the hymns, the responses, listens to the soaring anthem by the choir.

In a small, simple church on a bleak prairie a group of faithful gather to worship. The organist strains at the pedals as the reeds flutter in the uncertain wind created from the tiny bellows. The music of a familiar hymn reminds the worshipers to join in the singing.

This is music which aids the devout in their worship. From the beginning of time music has served to glorify God. The great composers — Bach, Mozart, Beethoven, Palestrina, Haydn, and hundreds of others — have used their God-given genius to help mankind sing praises to God.

Without music worship would seem dull and uninspired. With music the soul acquires wings and joins the angelic choirs. The majesty and glorious beauty of God become a reality through the office of music.

Whether it is a world-famous symphony orchestra playing a soul-stirring symphony or whether it is a little child seated at a piano playing a simple Sunday school hymn, music is one of God's most glorious means for bringing His children closer to Him.

MY PRAYER

Almighty God, I thank Thee for Thy magnificent creation of glorious music. Amen.

In the reverent quiet of the church I see the pastor facing the altar on which the Communion vessels gleam on the white fair linen. The Words of Institution come to me down the corridors of the centuries: "This is My body . . . given for you. . . . This is My blood . . . shed for you . . . for the forgiveness of sins."

My head is bowed, and in my mind's eye I see again that solemn scene in the upper room in Jerusalem during Jesus' last week of suffering and humiliation.

This is His last meal with His disciples, His friends. For about three years they have been closely associated in a life of learning and ministry. Now they will soon be parted. How can these friends remember Him? The Lord Jesus gives them a last testament, one which they will never forget and one which they are to use during the rest of their lifetime and which all believers are to use.

And so He institutes the Holy Communion. But it is even more than a last will. It is a sacrament, a means, a sacred act by which the forgiveness of sins is made sure to me and to all believers. In this sacrament I receive the body and blood of my Lord Jesus Christ. I receive the forgiveness of sins. I receive the strengthening of my faith in Him, in His life, in His work. Through this sacrament I become doubly sure that the day will come when I shall be reunited with Him in heaven.

As I reverently approach the altar, I am aware also of the vast fellowship of believers both of the past and of the present who believe as I do about my Savior. To me it seems that an unseen host of Christians from the days of the disciples until now are present with me and my fellow believers at the Lord's Table.

Holy Communion! I thank my heavenly Father for this blessed gift.

Often I wish I could remember the day of my baptism, for this was the most important event in my life. Naturally, I cannot remember this day because I was a tiny infant when my parents brought me to the church where I was baptized into the Christian faith.

Even though I cannot recall the physical details of my baptism, nevertheless the results of this event have been with me throughout my life. These results will continue to be with me until I leave this world to live in heaven with my Savior.

Through the Sacrament of Baptism I have been born again into the Kingdom of which Jesus is the Ruler. This is the way I entered that Kingdom; for Jesus Himself said: "Truly, truly, I say to you, unless one is born of water and the Spirit, he cannot enter the kingdom of God," John 3:5.

Perhaps it may seem strange that God uses water in this sacrament, for water is such an ordinary, everyday thing. The important thing to remember is that the water used in baptism does not of itself accomplish our rebirth, but it is the Word of God, which is used with the application of the water, and *faith,* which relies and trusts in that Word, that accomplishes this wonder. The Lord Jesus used a simple means to convey grace. The water alone has no spiritual power. In the words of St. Paul it is a "washing of regeneration and renewing of the Holy Ghost" when it is joined with God's Word.

Every time little children are brought to the baptismal font I say a special prayer for them. I pray that as they grow up they may also gratefully remember their baptism and that God's Holy Spirit will keep them firm and steadfast in their baptismal grace as new creatures.

FOR MEDITATION

Read St. Paul's statement thoughtfully: "For as many of you as were baptized into Christ have put on Christ," Galatians 3:27. Question: How do I best clothe myself with Christ?

Be faithful unto death, and I will give you the crown of life. Revelation 2:10

When I think about my confirmation two important facts stand out. These facts are deeply impressed on my mind and heart; and I hope with God's help I shall never forget them.

The first fact is that in preparation for my day of confirmation I had the opportunity to make a careful and systematic study of God's Word. Under the guidance of my pastor I, together with my friends in the confirmation class, learned about the teachings of the Holy Bible. I discovered again why I am a sinner and also how often I sinned. I also learned about God's love to me in the sending of His Son Jesus Christ, who is my personal Savior. These were only a few of the important things I learned. There were many more. Above all, I learned that for the rest of my life I will have to continue to be a student of Holy Scripture because there is always something important to be learned.

The second important fact about my confirmation is the solemn promise I made before the altar that I would remain loyal to my God and to my church through all the years of my life. In the presence of my parents and the congregation the pastor asked me whether I believed the teachings of the Bible and whether I intended to remain faithful. I answered that with the help of God I would remain true even though this loyalty could cost me my life.

This is a promise which I intend to keep not just on those days when it is easy to be a Christian, but it is a promise that I shall keep all the days of my life.

I firmly believe that if I remain true, God's promise to me will also come true: "Be faithful unto death, and I will give you the crown of life."

What is the most expensive thing in the world? Several high school students on their way home from school were discussing this question. One said, "My guess is an acre of ground on Wall Street in New York."

Another said, "I say a pound of finished diamonds."

The third student said, "A human life because once it's gone no one can restore it."

Just then they walked by their church, and one of the students said, "I guess we're all wrong. That's the most expensive thing in the world." He pointed to the cross over the entrance to the church.

The student was right. Here is how expensiveness is involved. That cross represents the grace of God, His love to all human beings. Grace means the relation of God to the sinner, the love which He shows to one who deserves no love.

This grace of God became very clear when God became a man in Christ. God died for the benefit of all men. God actually gave His Son into the hands of wicked men who crucified Him. By dying for the sins of mankind Jesus earned heaven for all those who believe on Him.

Grace means that God extends mercy to the sinner. But the sinner does not deserve this mercy. It is a gift of God. St. Paul eloquently describes this amazing fact when he writes, "Even though we were dead in our sins, God, who is rich in mercy, because of the great love He had for us, gave us life together with Christ — it is, remember, by grace and not by achievement that you are saved — and has lifted us right out of the old life to take our place with Him in Christ in the heavens." Ephesians 2:5, 6 (Phillips)

MEDITATION

Some of Christendom's greatest hymns are based on the theme of grace. Choose one hymn devoted to grace, and meditate on it.

God demands that everyone be perfect. He does not tolerate compromises but asks that purity, sinlessness, perfection be found in all His human creatures.

This is a staggering demand placed upon people. If we are honest, we must admit our inability to meet God's demands. We need, therefore, forgiveness for all that is wrong with us.

Christians believe that God Himself stepped into this breach between the holy God and sinful men. God took upon Himself the "weight of human wrongdoing." God offers free forgiveness to man through Jesus Christ, who paid for our sins by suffering and dying on the tree on Calvary.

Forgiveness comes through this Savior, to whom we come with our shame, our sins, our terrible load of evil. Jesus Christ lifts this off our shoulders and carries it for us. The price of this forgiveness is free. It is the gift of God to everyone who believes that Jesus Christ came into the world to save people and to give them forgiveness.

Tell God the story of your life, its sorry tale of sins. Tell God in detail, naming the sins one by one, how you have wandered from the path He wishes you to travel. Express true and deep sorrow over these sins. Ask God to forgive you, not because you are a good person or that you deserve such forgiveness. Ask God to forgive you because He loves you in His Son Jesus Christ.

The way of happiness in life is through knowing that your sins are forgiven.

FOR MEDITATION

"It is through the Son, at the cost of His own blood, that we are redeemed, freely forgiven through that full and generous grace which has overflowed into our lives." Ephesians 1:7 (Phillips)

When we are young, we want to grow older because then we will be able to make decisions for ourselves. The strange thing is that there comes a time in life when we have a fear of growing too old. The kind of age we live in seems to place a special value on remaining youthful. Girls especially may have a fear of growing older. They feel they may no longer be attractive.

There is a positive and a negative aspect to growing old. The negative aspect of growing old consists in closing the mind to new ideas, in refusing to see new challenges in living, in scoffing at new inventions or new theories without studying them.

The positive aspect of growing old means the acquiring of greater maturity of mind. With the passing of each year we use the judgments and values we have acquired and make them serve us in studying present-day problems. We also begin to have a greater appreciation of our parents and of the achievements of all the generations which have preceded us. Our admiration and love of God acquire depth and better understanding.

Growing old should always mean for the Christian growing up to greater heights of faith and love. This kind of growing old is not a physical process but a mental and spiritual one. Through prayer and through the study of God's Word, growing old becomes a daring adventure in which we cross new horizons every day. We become explorers. We look forward to the dawn of each day because this day gives us an opportunity to grow into more mature Christians.

A wise man once said, "The wrinkles on my face are purely physical. I shudder to think of the day when I have wrinkles in my mind. Then I will be truly a horrible 'old man.' "

MEDITATION

Think about these words of Paul: "We are meant . . . to grow up in every way into Christ, the Head." Ephesians 4:15 (Phillips)

The feeling of failure hits people in a variety of ways. Some feel deeply depressed when they realize they have failed in some particular job. Some become quite angry and rave about the unfairness of the world in general.

When you receive a failing grade in an examination or in a subject at the end of a semester, you are likely to blame the teacher, lighting conditions in the classroom, a bad cold you may have had, other school activities. The tendency is quite often to lay your failure on everyone and everything except yourself.

There are several ways to look at failure. One is to regard failure as a challenge to do better the next time. Failure in an examination means redoubled effort for the next examination. Say to yourself, "No excuses this time."

Another way to regard failure is as an opportunity to take another look at your goals in life. Suppose you decide to be a brilliant violinist. You practice for weeks and months and years. Try-out time comes for the position of first violinist in the school symphony orchestra. To your dismay, you do not get the position. You are overwhelmed with the feeling of failure, forgetting that perhaps the Lord never intended you to be a superb violinist.

Use failure creatively. Many great novelists had their first novels rejected by scores of publishers. Instead of giving up, they continued to write until they succeeded. Scientists, inventors, composers, artists have failed many times. They used these failures as a stimulus to greater and better efforts.

From the human point of view Jesus was a "failure." His crucifixion seemingly marked the end of a promising career. Yet out of this "failure" God's love brought about the resurrection and the entire march of faith.

"We know that in everything God works for good with those who love Him." Romans 8:28

One of the exciting facts about Paul was that he sang hymns when he was in jail. The other prisoners must have listened in amazement. There was nothing about Roman jails to make anyone want to burst forth into song. Jails were places for gloomy meditation.

Whether Paul and his friend Silas sang in tune and in harmony is omitted from the account. The important fact is to remember that in the hour of imprisonment they lifted their voices in song. Luke, who several times mentions in Acts that Paul and the early Christians spent time in singing, does not say what hymns those believers sang. Possibly they were psalms set to music, or hymns composed by early Christian poets.

This mysterious quality of the faith-increasing and strengthening power of hymns is hard to analyze. Sit around a campfire some late summer evening. Join in the singing of some of the great and favorite hymns. Your heart is stirred by this experience in a way which you will never forget. In the home, as the family gathers around the piano to sing hymns, the experience is equally unforgettable. Joining in this kind of song knits the family closer together.

Who can ever forget the lift which the spirit receives when an entire congregation joins in the singing of a powerful hymn of praise and worship to the Lord? It is as though our souls take wing and soar into the heavens.

The believers in the Old and the New Testament knew the beauty and power of hymns. They sang on many occasions. Through hymns they had another avenue of expressing the many aspects of their faith, even as we do today.

MEDITATION ASSIGNMENT

List your favorite three hymns in these spaces. As you read them silently, hum their melodies. _____

_____

_____

Next to parents and brothers and sisters, my pastor stands closest to me. He is my spiritual shepherd. He baptized me, and thus through the power of the Holy Spirit I became a child of God.

My pastor opened up to me the wisdom and the greatness of God's Word in the days of instruction preceding my confirmation. From him I learned the mighty truths about my soul's salvation. From him I learned how God hates sin but loves the sinner. From him I began to understand many of the mysteries of the Holy Bible. He made clear that which was complex and difficult.

When I was discouraged or troubled, my pastor consoled me. He listened to my problems and guided me in the proper ways to live and to think. When heartaches came to my family, my pastor was present to console us with the heavenly promises which God has given to His people. My pastor's prayers carried my family through its darkest hours.

Sunday after Sunday I listen to my pastor explain the meaning of the Holy Bible. As he stands in the pulpit and expounds the Word of God my faith is deepened and strengthened. His insights and his understanding of my needs help me to become a more devout child of God.

Each Sunday, as my pastor faces the congregation and pronounces the forgiveness of sins upon all of us in the name of the Triune God, a special feeling of calm and quiet joy comes over my soul. I know that he is speaking in the place of my Savior Jesus Christ.

The example of my pastor's life of service and dedicated devotion to other people encourages me to live, with God's help, a better Christian life. God bless my pastor!

PRAYER FOR MY PASTOR

O God, bless my pastor in his work as the shepherd of many souls. I ask this for the sake of Jesus Christ, my Savior. Amen.

You can now hope for a perfect inheritance beyond the reach of change and decay, "reserved" in heaven for you. 1 Peter 1:4 (Phillips)

The glorious fact about the Christian faith is that we know there is another life beyond the grave. When we must part from those whom we love, we feel an aching void. Our grief is deep and shattering. But above and beyond this grief is the hope of heaven. This hope surmounts the sorrows of this life.

What is heaven like? Words are inadequate to express its beauties. John in Revelation has written beautiful descriptions of heaven, but even these are not completely adequate. He uses words like crystal, jasper, gold, emerald, carnelian, amethyst, chrysoprase to convey the glory of our destination after death.

The most glorious aspect of heaven is that we shall dwell with God in this majestic holy city, a place where "God will wipe away every tear from their eyes, and death shall be no more, neither shall there be mourning nor crying nor pain any more, for the former things have passed away," Revelation 21:4.

Everything in this world will eventually rot or fade or wither or completely vanish. The mountains are impermanent. The seas can dry up. Human beings grow old and change. All pleasures eventually grow tiresome. All earthly things are impure, but heaven remains forever. Heaven will never grow tiresome or stale. It will always be a place of infinite delight and wonder.

Heaven is ours through the mercy of God in Jesus Christ. Heaven is ours without cost. God gives heaven to us.

MY PRAYER

Jesus, in mercy bring me to that dear land of rest. Amen.

There are few decisions more important than the decision we make about the work we shall do in our life. Choosing a vocation is difficult and necessary. It is difficult because there are so many factors to take into consideration. It is necessary because we know we want to lead useful lives.

Prayer is highly important as you go about the task of choosing a vocation. Ask God for help and guidance so that what you select as your life's work will be both pleasing to Him and useful to your fellow man.

Ask the advice of your parents. They know you better than anyone else. They have your best interests at heart.

Consult your pastor, who also knows you well and is concerned about your welfare. Ask your teachers, too, for their opinions.

Draw up a list of your strong and weak character points. Make a check list of your talents and your desires.

After you have done all these things, meditate on the meaning of your life in relation to your Savior. Remember what God says through His servant Peter: "Serve one another with the particular gifts God has given each of you, as faithful dispensers of the magnificently varied grace of God." 1 Peter 4:10 (Phillips)

MY PRAYER

Almighty God, send me out into life, not for cheap things and not for self but to do battle for Thy purposes. I ask Thee not for easier tasks, but for strength equal to my tasks. I ask Thee not for a smooth life. Make real to me, O God, the nobility of work. Help me always to see the joy in working for Thee to Thy glory and the welfare of my neighbor. In Jesus' name. Amen.

A man once said, "Money is the most powerful thing in the world."

His friend replied, "It's powerful in two ways: it can either send your soul to hell; or it can be the greatest servant in the world."

Money can buy false friends, and it can make enemies. It can buy a house, and it can buy clothes. It can buy you protection, and it can buy you the chrome-decorated modern car. If you have enough money, you can buy almost anything in the world.

But there are also things money cannot buy. These are some of the things money can never buy:

True friendship		A happy home
Love	Honor	Heaven

Money is a means which God has given to us for various purposes. Through money we are able to keep ourselves alive. Through money we can help build the church by sending out missionaries, erecting chapels, printing Bibles, establishing schools and colleges.

We are judged by the way we use our money. If we regard money as the end of everything, God judges us as poor stewards. If we think of money as a way to achieve God's purpose in the world, God approves. Money in and by itself never sent anyone to hell. It is the love of money which endangers the soul and all of spiritual life. This love of money is at the bottom of all evil, according to the apostle Paul.

The crisp green paper dollars we hold in our hands are the means to make life possible. They are not to be hoarded for their own sake. Use money. Do not let money use you.

MY MEDITATION

Study the rich fool in Luke 12:15-21.

The years have passed swiftly since that last day in October 1517, when Martin Luther challenged the church of his day to begin reforming. Since that day wars have been fought, learned councils have been held, thousands of books have been written — all because one man had become very angry over the abuses in Christendom.

Martin Luther has been called God's angry man by enemy and friend. His enemies accuse him of disturbing the peace. This is the same accusation hurled at Paul and Silas and Peter and a host of other great defenders of the faith. His friends say he had every right to be angry, because the Gospel message had grown fainter and fainter through the years. Martin Luther was angry for the simple reason that every person in the world was entitled to hear the Gospel from the church. He decided to do something about it.

Martin Luther wanted people to hear about God's love. In a sermon on the beautiful text from 1 John 4:16, "God is Love," he declared: "God's love is so clear that any man must see and grasp it if he will but open his eyes. For the gracious gifts of God stand every day before your eyes whichever way you look: the sun, the moon, and the heavens filled with light; the earth full of leaves, grass, and corn, and many kinds of plants, prepared and given to us for food. . . . And over and above all this He gave His beloved Son for you and through His Gospel brought Him home to you, to help you in every grief and dire affliction."

Hang out the flags for this angry man; blow the trumpets in his honor. The world needs angry men like Martin Luther.

A REFORMATION CHALLENGE

"The one thing needful is that we trust in our Lord Jesus Christ and believe in His Word." — *Martin Luther*

But about midnight Paul and Silas were praying and singing hymns to God while the other prisoners were listening to them. Acts 16:25 (Phillips)

Prisons are pretty uncomfortable and unhappy places. They were even worse in the days when the apostles were thrown into jail for being Christians. More often than not they were gloomy dungeons, damp, filthy, overrun with insects and rats. It was impossible to find a clean place to lie down. It was just as impossible to expect the jailer to provide the prisoners with a decent meal.

The early Christians were quite familiar with these jails. Many of the apostles spent considerable time in them. It's interesting to note that when Paul and his friend Silas were thrown into jail for disturbing the peace, they did not bemoan and bewail their sorry plight. They prayed and sang hymns.

Luke does not say whether Paul or Silas were good singers or whether they sang in pitch or what kind of hymns they sang. Presumably they sang some of the psalms and perhaps some very early Christian hymns. The point is: these men sang when they might have complained to God that they were getting a raw deal out of being missionaries. Another point is: their fellow inmates listened to Paul and Silas sing. This must have been quite an experience for them, and undoubtedly they wanted to know what made prisoners want to sing.

You don't generally sing when you are blue or depressed. Paul and Silas bubbled over with a zest for life because they were Christians. They were absolutely sure that God loved them in Jesus Christ. And so they sang even in jail.

TRY THIS

The next time you feel sorry for yourself sing a hymn of praise.

Quite often the modern father is an object of pitying laughter. At least, many radio and television plays picture father as a poor simpleton who can barely make his way through life's thousand and one complications. That he manages to survive at all is always a minor miracle. If it were not for the cleverness of a bright son and a brilliant daughter, poor father would be lost.

This down-grading of father is an unfortunate trend of our times. It's high time someone began a campaign to restore prestige to fatherhood. The fact is that the twentieth-century young Christian ought to set the pace in helping father receive rightful and honorable recognition.

Fathers may appear to their children as being queer creatures who work all day long and come home at night all tired out. To teen-agers fathers may seem like strange ogres who refuse to give permission to use the family car or who moan about the rising cost of shoes.

Fathers apparently don't have the ability to communicate their love for their children. For the truth is, fathers will go to great lengths to make life a more pleasurable experience for their sons and daughters. The deep abiding affection fathers feel may not often be expressed in eloquent language, but this love is frequently demonstrated in the kindly things a father does for his children.

One of the most tragic instances of a heartbroken father is the well-remembered incident when Absalom turned traitor on his own father. Absalom was killed, and when David heard the news of his unfortunate son's death, his shattering cry of love, "O my son Absalom, my son, my son Absalom! would God I had died for thee, O Absalom, my son!" has come down the years as a symbol of a father's poignant love for his children.

A PRAYER FOR MY FATHER

Heavenly Father, give me a growing sense of love for my father, even as Jesus loved Thee. Amen.

This is what a fighting marine told his chaplain during the bitter fighting in Korea: "Once I happened to walk past my parents' bedroom, and looking in I saw my mother kneeling beside the bed. The next morning I told her that I saw her kneeling, and I asked her what she was praying about. She said, 'I was praying for you, son.' I've always remembered this about my mother. She prayed for me when I was a small boy, and I know she is praying for me now. I know I should be afraid, but as long as I know she is praying I am certain that God will be with me. She is a wonderful mother. You may be sure that I ask God to be with her too."

There are times when mothers exasperate us. They always seem to be worrying. They worry about our health and about how we dress. They worry about our school work, and they worry about the friends we associate with. Mothers continue to worry even when their sons and daughters are grown men and women.

This is the nature of mothers. For their worrying is one way they have of expressing their love for us. This love is also shown for us when they teach us our first prayers. They are the first ones to tell us about the love of God in the Savior. Their concern and kindness cover us like sheltering wings.

One of the memorable sentences which Jesus spoke while hanging on the cross dealt with His concern for His mother. He asked John to care for her when He said to him, "Behold your mother!"

This love and honor Jesus paid to His mother is an example for every Christian to imitate and to cherish.

A PRAYER FOR MY MOTHER

Bless, O God, my mother. Guard her going out and coming in. Keep her always free from sin and safe from danger, and may she always safely rest in peace and quietness. In Jesus' name. Amen.

There is a charming old Italian tale, "The Wooden Bowl," about little Robertino, who loved his grandfather very much. One night at supper grandfather dropped his cup because his hands shook. The poor old man was banished to the kitchen and given a wooden bowl to eat out of. Robertino observed this and felt very sad. He took a small piece of wood and began to whittle it.

"What are you making, Robertino?" asked his mother fondly.

"I'm making a wooden bowl for you to have when you grow old and are a grandmother," answered Robertino.

The parents were too ashamed to meet Robertino's eyes. Then the mother took grandfather's arm and led him back to the table in the dining room and stood near him and helped him as he ate his supper.

Some of life's most precious moments are those spent in the company of grandfather and grandmother. Their kindliness, their devotion to their church and home, their memories which seem to go back toward far distant horizons make them fascinating people to talk to. Life would be rather dull if one associated only with a particular age group. By getting to know grandparents better one has contact with people whose experiences in a long lifetime have mellowed them and given them insights into life's problems which young moderns do not have.

Reverence for old age is an earmark of a high civilization. Holy Scripture repeatedly reminds Christians that they are to honor parents also when they have grown old. This would also include our grandparents.

MEDITATION SUBJECT

My grandfather and grandmother.

PROJECT

Write a letter to a grandparent.

The word sister is one of the most meaningful in the English language. In some English-speaking countries sister is used to designate a nurse or a deaconess. These are professions which demand devotion and selfless service.

I am always reminded of this when I think of my sisters. When I was very young, my mother frequently entrusted me to their care. They were always kind and thoughtful. As I grew older I learned to value my sisters' love for me.

I like to think of the relationship of Mary and Martha, two sisters, and their brother Lazarus. This was a home which the sisters kept functioning for their brother. Perhaps this family had lost the parents years ago, and now the sisters were determined to keep the family together. It was a home where the sisters were concerned about the Word of God. They loved the Savior. They welcomed Him as a guest.

When their brother died, they immediately asked Jesus to help them in their hour of sorrow. Martha was so overcome with grief that she reproached Jesus for not being in the home at the time of Lazarus' fatal illness. Very gently Jesus told her, "Your brother will rise again." Shortly after this Martha made the wonderful confession, "I believe that you are the Christ, the Son of God."

My sisters will always be for me a precious possession. I thank God for the gift of sisters. I pray always that I will bring no shame to my sisters. I shall defend their honor at all times, and I shall be gentle and courteous toward my sisters. The relationship I exhibit toward my sisters will later on be reflected in my relationship to the girl who will be my wife.

FOR MEDITATION

Read John 11:1-44. Question: How did the presence of Jesus Christ strengthen the relationship between brother and sisters?

Men or women may be old and in the shadow of their last years on earth, but somehow in talking about past memories you will hear this statement: "I remember my brother, who was kind to me when I needed help."

This is the joy to be found in Christian families, this affection of brother for brother or sister for brother. The note of pride is always to be detected when a person begins a sentence with "My brother . . ."

There are countless incidents in the Bible of the relationship between brothers. It is significant that one of the most brutal incidents in the history of mankind took place when Cain murdered his brother Abel. On the other hand, Jonathan and David, who were not brothers in the flesh, nevertheless considered themselves as brothers. When Jonathan lost his life, David's mournful cry over the loss of his "brother" has remained as one of the most eloquent testimonies to the beauties of the brotherly relationship. His cry of anguish in 2 Samuel 1 still touches the heart of everyone who reads it.

The Savior made the word "brother" a word of special significance, too, when He constantly spoke of those who believed in Him as being brethren or in the bond of brotherhood. Today Christians still speak of their fellow believers as brothers in the faith.

This high word of tribute to a human relationship makes doubly precious our relationship to the brother or brothers we may have in our homes. We are bound by the ties of common parenthood. We remember many common experiences. The joys and sorrows, the laughter and the tears of childhood and youth tie us in a bond that lasts until the end of time. "He is my brother" is a sentence of joy and pride.

MY PRAYER

Dear God, teach me to value my brother as a very special gift from Thy hands. May his and my relationship to each other always be one of loving kindness; for the sake of Jesus, my true Brother. Amen.

There are many happy customs connected with birthdays. There is a special birthday cake. Friends and family members give gifts. Many times there is even a party to celebrate the birthday.

At one high school, students always make an elaborate poster to hang on the locker of the person celebrating a birthday. All the students who pass by the locker autograph the elaborately decorated poster.

In a church office the employees observe this custom on their birthdays: The person who celebrates a birthday purchases a box of chocolates which are then shared with all the office members.

Birthdays are happy occasions for many reasons. Perhaps one reason is that when we observe our birthday we have passed another milestone in life and have reached another point in our march to adulthood.

The Christian is happy when he celebrates a birthday because he knows that God has been with him for another year. There may have been problems, even griefs in the past year, but the Christian also knows that God's protecting hand has been over him.

The Christian also knows that with each birthday another step has been taken toward that time when he will be united with the Lord Jesus Christ in heaven.

And so when a birthday is celebrated, every Christian asks God to forgive the follies and sins of the past year. The Christian also prays that God's grace will be as generous and merciful as it has been in the year just passed.

PRAYER ON MY BIRTHDAY

Lord, teach me always to live each day in Thy presence. May I always turn to Thee in sorrow and joy. Forgive my sins of the year just passed, and be with me as I enter a new year in my life. I ask this in Jesus' name. Amen.

"A teacher affects eternity," wrote the noted American historian Henry Adams. "He can never tell where his influence stops." St. Paul proudly referred to Gamaliel, the famous Jewish teacher, who was a highly learned man. St. Paul studied under this Gamaliel and acquired a deep knowledge of the Law.

My teacher in grade or high school exerts a profound influence on my life. This influence can be either direct or indirect. An inspired teacher can open up new avenues in the exciting adventure of learning. Sometimes a teacher can strike a spark in a pupil who later goes on to mighty achievements.

The truly dedicated Christian teacher can shape the future of the students in a wonderful manner. This kind of teacher arouses the desire in the students to become useful citizens who are aware at all times of their responsibilities to God and man.

As I think of the many teachers I have had in my school years, I remember especially my algebra teacher. One day I was completely lost in a complicated equation. I approached my teacher for advice or help. She welcomed me with a smile and said that at one time algebra had baffled her too. Then without hesitation she explained to me the proper method to use to solve the problem. The last thing she said as I was leaving, "I can't do your problems for you, but I can show you how to analyze them."

Since then I have applied this remark to all kinds of problems: personal, religious, educational. In matters of faith I have learned that I cannot do my problems myself, but if I turn to Scripture I see my problems not only analyzed but also solved.

PRAYER FOR MY TEACHER

Dear God, give my teacher wisdom and patience in dealing with me as a student. Amen.

Abraham . . . was called the friend of God. James 2:23

You are My friends if you do what I command you. John 15:14

A friend loves at all times. Proverbs 17:17

Once upon a time three men were talking about the past. They had not see one another since they were young men ready to begin their careers. After they had talked about the days of long ago, the first said rather expansively, "I've made a lot of money since then. I have a controlling interest in three major aircraft corporations."

The second said, "I have my own law firm, and I have important contacts in government. I have a direct wire to some of the most influential government people."

There was silence. The two men looked at the third. Finally, the first man asked, "Well, what have you got? After all, it's been a long time since graduation."

The third man looked uncomfortable for a moment. Then he brightened and said, "I don't suppose you fellows would count this as very much, but I have friends."

"A strange answer," the first man said.

"No," the third man replied. "For instance, I count God as my Friend. It's true He hasn't blessed me with corporations and law office, but He has given me peace of mind, faith, a sense of wonder over His majesty. Jesus Christ, His Son, is my Friend. Then I have dozens of other friends, the kind you might count as unimportant: the bus driver, my butcher, the corner cop, my pastor, yes, my children also. You know, it's a wonderful feeling knowing that I have all these friends. Don't forget: you are my friends too."

FOR MEDITATION

Think about friendship, starting with these words of the Lord Jesus: "Greater love has no man than this, that a man lay down his life for his friends," John 15:13.

The endless search for happiness is perhaps mankind's oldest quest. A wise Frenchman long ago said, "The thirst after happiness is never extinguished in the heart of man."

What people do to achieve this happiness is sometimes quite astonishing. A man who sat on a flagpole for more than three weeks said, "I am happiest when I am sitting up here."

Some men find happiness in the establishment of a large bank account; others believe that happiness may be found in power over other people's lives. Many girls believe that they would be the happiest people in the world if they were the most beautiful. Boys frequently think that ownership of a fast and shiny automobile would make them happy.

Jot down on these lines what you feel will make you a happy person. _____

_____

_____

Happiness can be defined in a variety of ways. It is peace of mind; it is a feeling of contentment; it is a satisfying emotion which comes from a good relationship with people; it is joy over gifts.

The noted translator of the New Testament, J. B. Phillips, translates the Beatitudes of Jesus in Matthew 5 with the word "happy." Thus the famous passage "Blessed are those who mourn, for they shall be comforted," is translated by Phillips, "How *happy* are those who know what sorrow means, for they will be given courage and comfort."

In the Bible, happiness and blessedness are interchangeable words in many places. Right here is the answer for the Christian who searches for happiness: "Blessed is everyone who fears the Lord, who walks in His ways," Psalm 128:1.

MY PRAYER FOR HAPPINESS

Bless me, O Lord, so that I may always be truly happy in Thee. Amen.

Out in the Montana range country one can see the horizon dotted at intervals with sheep wagons. Here the sheepherder and his dog live a good part of the year watching and guarding the huge flocks. The sheepherder knows no moment of relaxation. A band of coyotes may suddenly sneak into the flock and rip apart the herd. A sudden snowstorm may arise. At that moment the sheepherder and his dog stand in danger of losing their lives while guiding the sheep to shelter.

One of the most beloved pictures in the Bible is that of the Good Shepherd. Jesus pictures Himself as a shepherd constantly on the alert for the welfare of His flock. He is concerned about each sheep. If one of the sheep strays from the flock, He hunts the wandering sheep diligently. There is no rest until the lost sheep is found.

Just as sheep in the Montana ranges can easily wander away and become lost in some hidden ravine, so the Christian, a member of Christ's flock, also has a tendency to wander and stray from the flock of Christ's people. Yet the Good Shepherd guides His sheep gently to safe and proper pastures. When the Christian would stray, Jesus leads. If life's storms leave the child of God staggering, blinded, uncertain, the Good Shepherd is present. He stops at nothing to help His sheep.

The Good Shepherd has given His life for me because He loves me. Jesus says, "I am the Good Shepherd. The Good Shepherd lays down His life for the sheep."

MY PRAYER OF CONFIDENCE

The Lord my Shepherd is,
I shall be well supplied.
Since He is mine and I am His,
What can I want beside?

There is a beautiful custom observed in a small English church. Beside every family pew is a tall candle. As the family enters the pew for the evening service, the candle is lit. Naturally, the more families present, the more light there is in the church.

Jesus tells Christians to let their light shine in a dark world. Quite often Christians even forget to light the candles of their faith. Christians are expected to light their candles, and the more Christians lighting their candles, the more light there will be in the world.

On every side there is so much that is evil. Man's wickedness and selfishness make the world a dark place to live in. The greater the sinfulness, the greater the blanket of darkness.

So many Christians feel a trifle ashamed of their faith. They act as though they had been trapped into doing something not quite proper. Other Christians may place their names on a church book attesting their membership, but their conduct is unchristian.

Jesus says the only hope of the world rests in Him. He wants those who have accepted Him as the Savior to light up a dark world. Light is brought into the world by Christians who show by their words and deeds that they are truly reborn in Him. If the world sees Christians unashamed of their faith, then others will also, through God's Holy Spirit, come to the Cross of Christ.

Lighted candles for Christ Jesus are truly necessary in a world of gloom and doom.

MY MEMORY VERSE

"Let your light so shine before men that they may see your good works and give glory to your Father who is in heaven." Matthew 5:16

To an inheritance which is imperishable, undefiled, and unfading, kept in heaven for you. 1 Peter 1:4

The most pathetic accounts in newspapers are quite often the stories of children or relatives quarreling over the inheritance left by parents. Sometimes families are split for years because one child received more money or property than the other. More ironical is the discovery that lawyers' fees or change in values has devoured the coveted inheritance before the estate could be settled.

Despite the unhappiness inheritances can frequently bring, people continue to quarrel over a material inheritance as though all hope of happiness depended on it. These quarreling people have the age-old delusion that material possessions will bring happiness or security or peace of mind.

As a Christian I, too, have an inheritance. But my expectation is entirely different. I know that there is no money, no land, no stocks and bonds. I have an inheritance which is a living hope because of Christ's resurrection.

I am an heir because I am a child of God. This inheritance will never perish; the passage of time cannot lower its value, nor can any legal twisting and turning take it away from me. No matter what the changing fortunes of life may bring to me, I have a reservation made in heaven, where I shall see my Savior face to face, Him whom I love.

MY MEDITATION

In Revelation 22:5 I read these words: "And night shall be no more; they need no light or lamp or sun, for the Lord God will be their light, and they shall reign for ever and ever." I thank my heavenly Father for the inheritance of a glorious heaven which will be mine in all eternity.

You shall be My witnesses. Acts 1:8

There is something strangely exciting about the Gospel. It is not just an idea. It is not just the tragic story of a man who fell into the hands of a group of legal crooks. The Gospel is not some ancient history which people who call themselves Christians have to study before they can become church members.

The Gospel is good news of a singularly special kind. The Gospel is the message which tells people about God's love for them. God proved this love by sending His Son Jesus Christ into the world. This Son suffered, died, and rose again for only one reason: that those who believe in Him might get to heaven.

Another wonderful fact about the Gospel is that it must be shared. Once a person believes in the Gospel he must immediately communicate his joy with others.

The Gospel is always in motion. The people who put the Gospel into motion are witnesses. Without witnesses the Gospel would be unknown. God uses witnesses to transmit His message of love to the world.

When Jesus said, "You shall be My witnesses," He laid a heavy responsibility on every Christian. This responsibility cannot be dodged, for the Christian knows that he must share what he has with the unfortunate person who does not know the Gospel.

THREE QUESTIONS FOR MEDITATION

How much time is left for me to witness to my classmates? (John 9:4)

Where shall I witness to Jesus Christ? (Matthew 28:19)

Have I ever been ashamed to witness? (Romans 1:16)

Perhaps the most explosive issue in the world today is not the hydrogen bomb but relations between people of different color. The white-skinned people mistrust the yellow-skinned race, and the black-skinned people do not like the brown-skinned people. Among Christians, too, this mistrust and even hatred is to be found. Truly, trying to be Christian in our race relations is an important task set before the church member of the twentieth century.

Christians must always remember that the love of God and the love of man are inseparable. As a distinguished Negro scholar has said, "When Jesus summed up the Law and the Prophets by urging man to love God first and his neighbor as himself, He was urging man to put God and man at the center of his life." Whoever hates a person of another color of skin no longer places God at the center of his thinking.

The white high school student who writes a nasty anonymous note to a fellow student who is a Negro or Mexican does not love his neighbor. He is hurting his neighbor. He is trying to gain an advantage over that neighbor who stands in need of love and understanding and kindness.

God must always be at the center of all the Christian's thinking and doing. Within that center which God occupies the Christian also places the neighbor — the person of a different skin color. Our love for God cannot be separated from our love for our neighbor.

Whether in the classroom or on the basketball court or in a recreational area, the Christian youth forgets the surface difference created by color. The Christian young person remembers that God loves all people.

FOR MEDITATION

Read 1 John 4:19-21. Ask yourself this question: "What does this mean to me in my life as a high school student?"

O eternal God, Ruler of all the earth, I bless Thee for my country. Thou hast made me, O God, an heir to the majesty of upthrust mountains, the green of wooded hills, the prairies rolling to their far horizons, the fertile valleys where the rivers run. Hear me as I bring to Thee the tribute of my grateful heart:

For the mighty width of land from bordering sea to sea,
I thank Thee, O Lord.

For endless fields where the grain harvests ripen, for orchards with their golden fruit,
I thank Thee, O Lord.

For cattle in the meadows, for wild things in the woods, for fish in the oceans and lakes and mountain streams, for homely creatures of the barnyard, and for the infinite beauty of winged birds,
I thank Thee, O Lord.

For rich ores hidden in the hills, for coal and oil and iron,
I thank Thee, O Lord.

For the strength and skill of all the multitude of toiling men on whom our life depends: on farms, in fishing fleets, in factories, and before the fires of furnaces and mills,
I thank Thee, O Lord.

For all the servants of the mind, for scholars and teachers, for authors and artists, and for all poets in word or deed who reveal the wideness and wonder of Thy world,
I thank Thee, O Lord.

Help me to be a faithful citizen of my country. Help me to be a good steward of all these riches. Give me strength to be firm in my love to Thee; through Jesus Christ my Lord. Amen.

Some men worship power, some worship security, some worship wealth or popularity. Through their acts these men show they place their faith and love in that which is apart from God.

The Christian also worships, but the Christian worships the true God, not the false gods of money, popularity, security. The Christian renders his devotion and adoration to the true God because he loves God and because he knows God expects such worship.

My worship reaches a climax on Sunday when I turn into the house of God and join my fellow believers in praising, adoring, and thanking God. I pray. I hear God's Word. I dedicate myself to God. I offer my gifts to God. I confess my faith in God. This is all part of my worship.

I worship God as my heavenly Father, my Creator. I worship His only-begotten Son, Jesus Christ, who loved me first and gave His life for me. I worship the Holy Spirit, who brought me to faith through Holy Baptism and still keeps me in faith.

My worship is both simple and complex. It is simple in the sense that I turn all my thoughts to God, the eternal One who never changes. It is complex because I not only believe in God but I also pray to Him and I confess my sins to Him. I marvel that God loves me despite my many shortcomings, that God cherishes me even though I am a sinner.

Hence my worship is also a constant giving of thanks for all that God has done for me. Truly the glory of worship is more precious to me than all other activities in the world.

MY COMMAND TO WORSHIP

"Oh, come, let us worship and bow down, let us kneel before the Lord, our Maker! For He is our God, and we are the people of His pasture and the sheep of His hand." Psalm 95:6, 7

Since printing began, the Bible has outsold and outcirculated every other book. An expert estimates that over 1,500,000,000 Bibles have been printed since 1500. Another expert estimates that 75,000 books about the Bible have appeared since the Reformation. These are staggeringly high figures and demonstrate the place the Bible holds in the life of mankind.

There must be a profound reason for the Bible's tremendous popularity. The reason may be stated very simply: God reveals Himself through a book. From the beginning of time men and women have wanted to know about God. What is He like? What does God say to people? Where is God in time of trouble? Then there are all the related questions: Who made the world? What about sin? Why do I have an inner voice which bothers me when I do wrong?

Presumably God could have told everything about Himself by some other means than words written or printed on a page. But He used words, and these words offer a detailed description of God, of man and his relationship to God, what man must believe about God, how much man needs God.

Thus through all the centuries man turns to the Bible, Holy Scripture, for a variety of reasons:

Information about God
Comfort in time of sorrow
Help when life becomes complicated
Joy in the life of Jesus Christ
Faith for this life and hope for eternity

MY PRAYER

May the light from Thy Book, O God, descend into my life and always display to me the Savior's boundless love. Amen.

One of the most saddening experiences one can have is to meet up with a person who says he is a Christian but seldom acts the part. This is lip-loyalty. Perhaps Judas Iscariot was such a person. He said he was a follower of the Savior. His betrayal of the Lord for thirty pieces of silver was horrifying proof that he did not act like a follower.

In a small town in Indiana there is a lovely church which is a perfect symbol of all we should not be. It is set off from the street, beautifully landscaped with the proper shrubbery. The passer-by is immediately impressed with the beautiful exterior. But when he enters the church, an opposite picture is obtained. The altar is wrecked, the windows are covered with cobwebs, the pulpit is tottering to one side. Everything is ready for collapse. The exterior deceived the visitor.

Those who call themselves Christians but do not act like Christians resemble this church. Their exteriors are beautiful, but their interiors — their deeds — are wrecks. These people use vile language, they get drunk, they are harsh with their families, they cheat in examinations, they tell lies, they seldom attend church, they hardly ever give to charitable causes. Yet they say they are Christians. But their deeds prove that their saying so is not true. They have merely the form of faith. The living presence of the Savior is far away.

Beware of landscape Christianity!

I MEDITATE ON —

"Faith without action is as dead as a body without a soul."
James 2:26 (Phillips)

The person who has the answer to the problem of human suffering would indeed be a genius of the first rank. Why must small children suffer the distortions of a crippling disease? Why must young men of promise be killed in war? Why must a happy home be broken up by disease and death? Why must there be war and the unspeakable suffering that comes in its wake?

The Christian has the best answer to this problem of suffering. The answer may not be satisfying in the fullest sense, since only heaven will be able to give the why and the wherefore. The best answer for the life in this world is in St. Paul's great passage from his Letter to the Romans: "We know that all things work together for good to them that love God."

Some heartache, some death, some bit of suffering may at first glance truly seem to have no purpose back of it. To the thoughtless person, God may sometimes appear to act in a whimsical manner.

When such a feeling does occur, it is well to remember that nothing happens to the Christian, especially suffering, without the Christian being benefited. If faith grew, if God came closer, if the love of Christ became more real, then suffering was not in vain. God says emphatically that everything that happens to a person happens for good. The answer may be delayed. Perhaps it may never come in this world. The final answer will be that all happened for good to those who loved God.

FOR THE HEART TO REMEMBER

What God ordains is always good.
He never will deceive me;
He leads me in His own right way,
And never will He leave me.
I take content, What He hath sent;
His hand that sends me sadness
Will turn my tears to gladness.

In his notable autobiography of several years ago, Jim Piersall, the very good outfielder formerly with the Boston Red Sox, described some of the various fears which made life miserable for him as a baseball player. He worried about success in hitting, in meeting the stiff big-league competition. The more he thought about his fears the more tensed up he became. Soon he lost his mental health. The rest of his story in *Fear Strikes Out* is a dramatic account of his recovery. He lost his fears or, at the very least, he was able to live with those fears as a Christian.

Every human being has fears. The Christian has fears, too, because the Christian is also a human being. One of the best ways to attack this problem of fears is to make a list of your fears. Take a pencil and a piece of paper, and jot them down as you would jot down a shopping list.

Here's some white space for you to note just three of your fears.

In this following white space, write out David's challenge to his fears. This is found in Psalm 56:3.

FOR MEDITATION

Thou knowest all my griefs and fears,
Thy grace abused, my misspent years;
Yet now to Thee with contrite tears,
Christ Crucified, I come. — *Joseph Barnby*

One of the most common of feelings is that of loneliness. You can feel lonely in a crowd in an evening traffic rush hour. You see the hundreds and thousands of people milling about you or dashing madly from one place to the next. You feel that there is no one in the crowd who cares about you.

There is the lonely feeling when you are alone in your room with your thoughts, with your problems, with your sorrows. It is at such moments that loneliness becomes as terrifyingly real as a towering ocean wave poised before it crashes upon you.

The feeling of loneliness is not unnatural. Everyone at some time or other in life has such a feeling. Various Presidents have said that they have felt like the loneliest men in the world as they sat in the White House thinking about decisions which had to be made the next day.

To be alone is as necessary for a human being as to be with a group of friends. In aloneness one can think and meditate quietly about the big and little problems of life. After such a time of being alone without the intrusion of people one can with renewed courage go back into the bustle of living.

Loneliness and the feeling of aloneness can become very creative factors in living by remembering this: the presence of God ought to become truly real and vital. When loneliness becomes a depressing factor, the image of David, lonely and sad in the wilderness of Judah, comes to mind. Instead of being filled with self-pity he sings joyously, "My mouth praises Thee with joyful lips, when I think of Thee upon my bed and meditate on Thee in the watches of the night; for Thou hast been my Help," Psalm 63:5-7.

MY MEDITATION

The Lord is with me in my hours of loneliness.

Remember, I am with you always, to the end of the world.
Matthew 28:20 (Phillips)

Where is the end of the world? The center of the ocean? The filthiest hole in Skid Row? A sea-front basement in Singapore? The death cell in Cook County Jail? These places are the end of the world for many people. And yet Jesus Christ is in these places. If I had to go to these places, I am confident God would find me.

Perhaps David wondered, too, whether God could be found in the ends of the world — in places distant and frightening. He wrote: "If I take the wings of the morning and dwell in the uttermost parts of the sea, even there shall Thy hand lead me, and Thy right hand shall hold me."

The end of my world isn't far away. Once it was the assembly halls of the high school where I faced the world alone for the first time. I thought that I had come to the end of the world. Once the end of my world was a college campus where I stood bewildered, scared, and homesick. Another time the end of my world was in a lonely Wyoming town where my car had broken down.

The ends of my world will always change. There will be many more times when I am alone, utterly lost and forgotten. But I also know this: wherever I go, when I go in faith, my Savior is beside me to give me His enduring strength and aid.

That's why I tell anyone — a hobo, a soldier, a mountain climber, a jet pilot: "You don't have to be afraid. You are never alone. Jesus Christ is with you always, even to the ends of the earth. How do I know? He made that His promise."

PRESCRIPTION FOR LONELINESS

Think of Jesus in the Garden of Gethsemane.
Think of Martin Luther facing his enemies.
Remember Jesus' promises.

Directly after this Jesus insisted on His disciples getting aboard their boat and going on ahead to the other side, while He Himself sent the crowds home. And when He had sent them away, He went up the mountain quite alone, to pray. Matthew 14:22, 23 (Phillips)

An Indian Christian friend said to me, "You Americans are always in a rush. You don't know how to be quiet. Do you ever have time to pray?"

There is certainly a great deal of truth in this observation. It is important to have a quiet time each day. If I don't make an effort to set aside a quiet time, then I find I forget to read God's Word, to pray, to meditate on His work.

Many times when I am busy I excuse myself by saying, "I attend church every Sunday. In the family circle we have our daily devotions. Surely this ought to be enough."

Then I recall this passage from St. Matthew which tells how Jesus left His busy life behind and went up into the mountains quite alone to pray. Here He could escape from the noise and confusion of everyday life and turn His attention to His Father. He had time and opportunity to pray. In this mountain solitude God could not be crowded out.

Every day I say to myself: "Today I must set aside some time for quiet meditation. This is the best way I have of being with God in undisturbed prayer."

The most remarkable fact is that those few moments spent with God in quiet give me courage and energy to face the noise and rush and excitement of the modern world.

MY PRAYER

Dear God, may I always remember to spend some quiet moments with Thee in prayer, in meditation, in wonder over Thy glory and love. Amen.

Sometimes when I see our crowded churches, I like to go back in memory to the days when there were no churches, no crowds, no eager Christians on the way to public worship.

I think instead of a crude drawing of a fish on an alley wall or on the pavement of a street in Rome or Naples. This sign of the fish was used by the Christians to convey a message to other Christians without the police being any wiser. Any Christian seeing this fish drawing knew that right within the vicinity a church service would be held.

Those were the days when being a Christian meant persecution. You dared not stand on a street corner distributing tracts which told about Jesus Christ. In the first century of the Christian church it was necessary quite often to be an underground Christian. You had to carry on your propaganda work for the faith in a subtle, almost secretive manner. Those early Christians must certainly have valued their faith. As a matter of fact, thousands lost their lives to the Roman government because they refused to change their loyalty from Jesus Christ to the emperor.

The Greek word for fish is ἰχθύς. The letters of this word are the initials of the words "Jesus Christ, God's Son, Savior." Like this, but using the capital letters now:

I is the first letter of the Greek word for Jesus.

X is the first letter of the Greek word for Christ.

Θ is the first letter of the Greek word for God's.

Y is the first letter of the Greek word for Son.

Σ is the first letter of the Greek word for Savior.

I am grateful for living in a time when I need not be an underground Christian. I ask God's Holy Spirit to give me courage and ability to testify openly to my faith in my Savior Jesus Christ.

Since the beginning of time men and women, young people and children have chanted the praise of nature, that beautiful world around us on every side. The roar of the waves crashing on the rocky New England coast, the mystic and quiet splendor of the California redwoods, the stormy crags of the Canadian Rockies — these and many other aspects of nature fill everyone with awe and wonder.

"The world is charged with the grandeur of God," sang the British poet Gerard Manley Hopkins. Truly, he who lives with nature or studies it even for a passing moment is almost inevitably drawn to the conclusion that there is a God; for God speaks to us also through the beautiful world He has created for our enjoyment.

David exclaimed rapturously, "The heavens declare the glory of God," Psalm 19:1. The Lord Jesus loved nature and all growing things. "Consider the lilies, how they grow," He said to His disciples. "They neither toil nor spin; yet I tell you, even Solomon in all his glory was not arrayed like one of these," Luke 12:27. Surely many times He contemplated the quiet beauty of flowers in the Palestinian countryside and expressed thankfulness to His heavenly Father for this wonderful gift. How many times He watched sunsets on the Sea of Galilee and absorbed the beauty. Our Lord loved the beauty of nature because here, too, God expresses Himself.

As I look upon nature, I ask that God constantly remind me of His glory and majesty. Without Him there would not be this world. With Him, the Creator, there is the sublime majesty of nature, an expression of His love for His children.

MEDITATION THEME

What does this mean to me? — "God created the heaven and the earth." Genesis 1:1

Absalom stole the hearts of the men of Israel. 2 Samuel 15:6

There are some people who will do almost anything to achieve popularity, for they think that being popular is the same as being liked. Certain kinds of people hire press agents to build up their popularity. These people, usually of the theatrical world, feel that as long as their names are mentioned in the newspaper gossip columns they have achieved their heart's desire: popularity.

This kind of popularity is wrong and is bound to bring only unhappiness and disillusionment. One of the classic instances of a young man who sought popularity is Absalom, one of David's favorite sons. Absalom wanted to be popular and therefore resorted to trickery to achieve this popularity. In the end, while he may have won temporary popularity, he found only tragedy in the cheap kind of popularity he sought. Through his popularity he hoped to hurt his father. It could be truly said in this instance what an English statesman said over two centuries ago: "Popularity is a crime from the moment it is sought."

High school students frequently brood through miserable hours over their lack of popularity. Quite often one is unpopular because one does not use dirty language or because one tries, with God's help, to be a conscientious Christian.

Do not worry about your popularity with your schoolmates. Be far more concerned about your popularity with God — your being well liked by Him as a humble Christian.

MY PRAYER

Dear God, let me never cast aside my Christian standards to achieve popularity. Give me courage to be unpopular for Christ's sake. Amen.

Among the many dramatic accounts of World War II experiences is the story of two American aviators, captured by the Japanese, who were to be beheaded. The executioner, knowing the aviators were Christians, felt they ought to have some Christian comfort as they faced death. In a nearby prison compound was a captured Christian missionary. The aviators' guard visited the missionary and asked him for a Bible. But the missionary had lost everything. He tried to recall some Bible passage which would be of special comfort to the aviators. At last he remembered the beautiful passage from John 14: "In My Father's house are many mansions; if it were not so, I would have told you. I go to prepare a place for you."

The missionary drilled the verse into the guard's memory and then told him to repeat those words to the two aviators. As the aviators were led to the execution scene, they repeated these words to each other and then continued with the Lord's Prayer.

These brave men faced death as true Christians. Although they were in the hands of the enemy, they knew that this enemy had no lasting power over them. They found hope in the knowledge that their Savior had preceded them. Jesus had ascended into heaven to prepare a place for them. These aviators may have had their moments of fear before the moment of death, yet deep within they had the certain faith that their Redeemer was awaiting them.

MY PRAYER

Be Thou my Consolation,
My Shield, when I must die;
Remind me of Thy Passion
When my last hour draws nigh.
Mine eyes shall then behold Thee,
Upon Thy cross shall dwell,
My heart by faith enfold Thee.
Who dieth thus dies well. Amen.

It is hard to smile when there are tears in the eyes. It is hard to appear hopeful when there is only grief in the heart. We are often resentful toward the person who tells us to keep a stiff upper lip when the aches of life are twisting like knives in our heart. There are many times when we feel that all is hopeless and that it is best to be a pessimist. When death or other sad news enters our lives, then we have the natural human reaction that all is worthless.

In the Old Testament, Job had such twentieth-century feelings. He feels desolate, abandoned, hopeless. Even his friends are against him. He feels that it is senseless to keep a stiff upper lip. Life is too rugged. Nature, he thinks, is far better off. He exclaims, "There is hope of a tree if it be cut down that it will sprout again and that the tender branch thereof will not cease." As for himself, he is sure that all is hopeless.

Job does not end on a note of despair. He does keep a stiff upper lip, that badge of courage, because he has a faith which will see him through the darkest days.

Job knows that above all the tragedies of the world God's hand is guiding the universe and even his own life. He firmly believes that God is with him through all trials. He knows that the day will come when he shall see his Redeemer face to face, when the pettiness and sorrow of his earthly life will be a forgotten memory in the presence of God's holy angels. This hope and faith give him the strength to keep that stiff upper lip.

SING THIS SONG WITH JOB

"For I know that my Redeemer liveth and that He shall stand at the Latter Day upon the earth; and though after my skin worms destroy this body, yet in my flesh shall I see God, whom I shall see for myself, and mine eyes shall behold, and not another." Job 19:25-27 (King James)

Be subject for the Lord's sake to every human institution.
1 Peter 2:13

The early Christians had every reason to hate or despise the government. The majority of these believers were victims of injustice, cruelty, dishonesty. If any of them had plotted for the overthrow of the government, humanly speaking, they would have been justified. Yet nowhere do we read about an apostle advising a revolution against the government. Instead the Christians were models of obedience.

To this day, Christians, if they are genuine and sincere in their faith, render the same kind of obedience and respect to the government. They are conscientious and sincere citizens.

Does a Christian pay his income tax because he is afraid of the penalty for not paying? Does the Christian answer the draft call for military service because he does not want to serve a term in a federal penitentiary?

Not if he takes his Christian faith seriously. God's Word points out the inescapable fact that Christians submit themselves to laws and government for the Lord Jesus' sake. Jesus loved us; He set an example of obedience. Instead of bringing shame upon Him, the Christian obeys because he loves the Savior. By Christian example, honor is brought to the faith. A godly attitude toward government will silence the criticisms of the unbeliever.

The Christian will also do everything in his power to improve the quality of government. The Christian will pray for his government. If the government is wicked, then the Christian attempts with God's help to improve the government.

The Christian always remembers that "it is God's will that by doing right you should put to silence the ignorance of foolish men," 1 Peter 2:15.

MY PRAYER

Heavenly Father, help me to be a conscientious citizen of my government. Amen.

A high school teacher said to her class, "We ought to act like Christians."

One of the students raised his hand and asked, "How do you act like a Christian?"

The teacher was quiet for a moment and then replied, "I suppose I could make a long speech on that subject. Instead of a speech, let this passage from Ephesians 4 be at least part of my answer: 'Be kind to one another, tenderhearted, forgiving one another, as God in Christ forgave you.' "

There is so much hatred in the world that it is a wonder people still manage to get along with one another. War or the threat of war opens many old wounds and creates many new ones. National and international tensions help develop unforgiving attitudes.

Frequently families let frazzled nerves get the upper hand. Real or imaginary wrongs create disturbances which destroy a peaceful and happy routine in the home. Brothers and sisters quarrel, and tears become more common than laughter.

Paul says, "Be tenderhearted." Why? Because that is the easy way out? Not at all. Remember that God for Christ's sake has forgiven our many sins. Think of the many times a Christian offends his God by his meanness, jealousy, bad temper, selfishness. Yet God loves us. He forgives sins for Christ's sake.

Therefore the Christian should love others. He should be kind, tenderhearted, forgiving even when it means that the other cheek might be slapped.

The Lord Jesus forgave the mean and wicked people who mocked Him, beat Him, crucified Him. He was tenderhearted. He remains the eternal Example to every Christian.

MY PRAYER

Lord Jesus, give me a tender heart toward all people. Amen.

Martin Luther said that prayer is the daily business of every Christian. In this daily communication with God the Christan grows stronger in faith and richer in understanding of God.

There are three aspects of the prayer life which, if remembered and practiced, will make praying a daily necessity.

First, prayers should be God-centered. Too many of our prayers center on our own problems and desires. We often think we know what is best for our own lives. We forget that God, who knows all things and knows what is best for us, may have a will completely different from our own. We need to follow Jesus' example, who encouraged His followers to pray: "Thy will be done."

Remember to pray for others before you pray for yourself. By praying for others you stifle your own selfishness, and your love for others constantly increases. Jesus prayed for others while He was in the death agony of the cross. Stephen prayed for those who were stoning him. Thomas More, just before he was led to death by his fellow Englishmen in the sixteenth century, asked the spectators to pray for the king who had ordered his execution. It is truly hard to pray for those who hate us and hurt us. But Jesus said, "Pray for those who persecute you."

Last of all, pray for yourself, for your own needs, for the solving of your own problems. Because we are such complicated beings with a thousand and one different wants, we are likely to pray for material blessings, such as money, health, happiness, jobs, success. Needed as these blessings are, it is of far greater urgency to pray that God would forgive us our sins for Jesus' sake. We should pray that our knowledge and understanding of God be constantly enlarged. And we always pray for God's grace in our lives.

A PRAYER ASSIGNMENT

Write down the names of three people, known or unknown to you. Pray for them, using their names in your prayers.

In the book *Searchlight on Peace Plans* we read that men have been making postwar plans for an enduring peace since 1306. For many centuries men have thought and dreamed of a day when there would be no more war but only peace among men. Every variety of peace plan has been proposed but, as history proves, those peace plans have gone down the drain. Nations have marched to war at almost regular intervals.

Most peace planners seem to forget the human heart and the part it plays in the progress of a nation. Within every human heart there is envy or hatred or jealousy. Ultimately this is what causes war.

St. John spoke truly and correctly when he said that if we cannot love our brother, whom we see, how can we love God whom we do not see. Jesus said that out of the heart proceeds all wickedness. We must first learn to love the neighbor who lives across the street. We must ask God for help to practice this love, for out of the heart proceeds hatred.

Instead of becoming cynical about our nation's plans for peace, Christians must pray that government leaders will be given courage and wisdom to carry out these peace plans. Christians need to ask God to soften the hearts of those who would plan war against other nations.

Everlasting peace on earth may be a distant dream, but this should never prevent Christians from working at the job of achieving peace. Above all, Christians must realize that God hears also their prayers for peace. In God's wisdom such prayers will be answered.

MY PRAYER FOR PEACE

Merciful God, I beseech Thee to help me live at peace with my neighbor. Even as I live at peace with my neighbor, give peace between nations. In Jesus' name. Amen.

Someone said, "If we could eliminate worrying from people's lives, there would be heaven on earth." Even sadder is the fact that Christians spend a great deal of valuable time worrying.

I worry about whether I will pass the semester exams. I worry whether my clothes look neat and presentable. I worry about my mother's health. I worry about getting a job during the summer months. I worry about not having enough money.

Isn't this strange? Actually, I ought to stop for a moment for some careful stock taking. Has God cared for me today? during the week? during the year? Did God's protecting hand ever leave me? I must honestly and believingly say: God has been with me. In a thousand and one ways His presence was in my life.

Therefore, why should I worry? My Savior has spoken most eloquently many times about His concern for me. He has assured me that the heavenly Father knows all the things I have need of.

A great Christian has said: "I do not take any worries to bed with me." Bishop Quayle tells of lying awake trying to hold the world together by his worrying. Then God said to him: "Now, William, you go to sleep, and I'll sit up."

I have resolved not to ruin the days and the months and the years which lie ahead of me by worrying. This time is too wonderful and too lovely to ruin with worries.

The reason my worries are no longer burdensome is to be found in the Savior's own words:

"Look at the birds in the sky. They never sow nor reap nor store away in barns, and yet your heavenly Father feeds them. . . . Don't worry at all then about tomorrow. Tomorrow can take care of itself! One day's trouble is enough for one day." Matthew 6:26, 34 (Phillips)

He said to them, "But who do you say that I am?" Simon Peter replied, "You are the Christ, the Son of the living God." Matthew 16:15, 16

MY MEDITATION

Recently I decided to ask a few fellow Christians, "What does Jesus mean to you?" For the most part, I received a puzzled look, followed by an embarrassed silence. Sometimes I seriously wonder whether this name hasn't taken on a vague and distant meaning in our lives. Then, too, I ask myself: Why should I or how can I be a living witness for Jesus if He isn't within my personal life — at this very moment? Surely for Christians, Jesus should have meaning. So I examined myself for an answer to the same stirring question.

To me Jesus is the truest and greatest friend that I or anyone else can possibly have. It's truly a reassuring thought to know that while Jesus was on earth He was a friend to sinners and that He promised to be with us always until the very end of the world. It brings me personal happiness and comfort to know that He is always present, always willing to listen, and always willing to help. I know that I can tell Him at all times of the joy, confusion, or depression that I feel, even while I'm walking to classes.

I know, too, that this greatest of friends does even more than guide me in the perfect life that He revealed and lived so many years ago, but that He also took upon Himself all my sins and died that He might be my Savior. He is the way to salvation. He completely understands my sinful nature and my inability to overcome sin, sickness, and death without Him. He is Love and Life for me, and in none other could I find this but in my Friend Jesus.

MY PRAYER

Heavenly Father, let me always remember how much Jesus means to me. He is my Savior, my Friend, Thy beloved Son. Amen.

In old Russia the walls of the Greek Orthodox churches had many images of saints. These icons were not placed there to worship but to recall to the congregation the great multitude of the redeemed now gathered about the heavenly throne worshiping God.

Worship of the true God within the company of a congregation is a highly moving experience because this is the family of God approaching the heavenly Father through Jesus Christ. This worship is expressed through the prayers either read by the pastor or spoken by the congregation. It is confessing the faith in one of the great creeds. It is hearing God's Word expounded to the congregation. It is joining in the mighty hymns of praise and adoration and exultation. By uniting with fellow believers in this act of worshiping God the individual believer's faith is strengthened. From true worship the Christian receives reassurance from God of the forgiveness of sins and the glorious grace which He has bestowed upon all believers.

Raymond Abba tells the well-known story of an English colonel in World War I who was stationed in a French village. This rather cynical colonel delighted in ribbing the old village priest. One Sunday morning the colonel passed the church as a handful of people were leaving the services. "Not very many in church this morning, Father, not very many." "No, my son, you're wrong," was the reply. "Thousands and thousands and tens of thousands!"

Truly, there is no greater or more wonderful human activity than to join with your fellow believers and with all the company of saints in glorifying God through worship.

MY MEDITATION

What does this mean to me? — "Therefore with angels and archangels and with all the company of heaven we laud and magnify Thy glorious name, evermore praising Thee and saying: Holy, Holy, Holy, Lord God of Sabaoth; Heav'n and earth are full of Thy glory."

The Declaration of Independence has changed the course of human history. Many books, such as *Mein Kampf* or *Das Kapital,* have been written which have altered men's ways of thinking and doing things. Some of these documents and books are known only to the scholar who knows his way through library stacks.

Towering over every document and book written by man, there is one book, one Word, which has done more to change the world than anything else ever written.

That Word, that Book, is the Bible, my Bible, the Word spoken by God through His chosen writers. Jesus, the Son of God, asks everyone to believe this Word. He who believes that Word becomes one of His disciples. I believe my Bible. Therefore I am a disciple of my Lord Jesus Christ.

The wonderful fact about the Bible is that all of the great, fundamental problems of life are answered in its pages. Why am I here in the world? Where am I going? Is there a God? What kind of God do I believe in? What is sin? Does God really care for me? Why must there be heartache and sorrow in the world? What is true happiness? What happens after death?

As I read my Bible I learn to know God's truth. I learn about God's Law and God's Gospel. I discover the terrible meaning of sin, and I discover the beautiful meaning of Calvary.

I have learned from my Bible how to be free from sin, doubt, and the judgment to come. I have learned from my blessed Bible that God forgives me my sins for Jesus' sake. I have discovered the happiness that comes from being free from guilt and having the hope of heaven always with me.

MY SONG

How precious is the Book Divine,
By inspiration given!
Bright as a lamp its doctrines shine
To guide our souls to heaven.

A noted theologian has made the significant comment: "The period of time that lies between the cradle and the grave is merely a small moment in the full life of a child of God."

I must realize that my life is but a small moment between birth and death. During this small moment I must adopt a particular attitude toward my life, my possessions, my job, the welfare of those around me.

During my small moment in the world I must through the guidance of the Holy Spirit do everything to the glory of God. I must be able to give a happy account of my stewardship of all things entrusted to me during this small moment.

All that I am comes from the hand of God. All that I have has been given to me by the Creator. During my small moment in this world I am a steward, a caretaker, of these possessions.

When I act according to this Scriptural truth, then I will be laying up treasures for myself in heaven. I am acting in a God-pleasing manner when I say, "All that I have and all that I am, O Lord, is Thine alone."

The small moment in this world will some day expand into that greater glory which is the goal of all Christians: heaven.

Truly, the advice which St. Paul gave to the rich applies also to me: "Tell them to do good, to be rich in kindly actions, to be ready to give to others and to sympathize with those in distress. Their security should be invested in the life to come, so that they may be sure of holding a share in the life which is permanent," 1 Timothy 6:18, 19. (Phillips)

MY PRAYER

Dear Lord Jesus, make the small moment of my life rich in love toward Thee. Amen.